To my wife, Åsa.

To my children: Ashley and Andrew.

In memory of my father, Joseph.

To my mother, Connie.

THE
Focused
CEO

THE Focused CEO

WHY SOME ORGANIZATIONS THRIVE AND OTHERS SPIN THEIR WHEELS

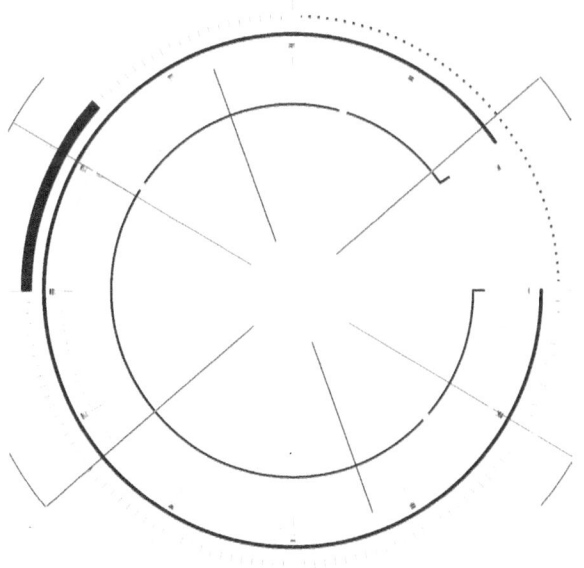

ANDY VASSALLO

The Focused CEO

Copyright 2020 © Andy Vassallo

All information, techniques, ideas and concepts contained within this publication are of the nature of general comment only and are not in any way recommended as individual advice. The intent is to offer a variety of information to provide a wider range of choices now and in the future, recognizing that we all have widely diverse circumstances and viewpoints. Should any reader choose to make use of the information contained herein, this is their decision, and the contributors (and their companies), authors and publishers do not assume any responsibilities whatsoever under any condition or circumstances. It is recommended that the reader obtain their own independent advice.

First Edition 2020

ISBN: 9798585899027

All rights reserved in all media. No part of this book may be used, copied, reproduced, presented, stored, communicated or trans¬mitted in any form by any means without prior written permission, except in the case of brief quotations embodied in critical articles and reviews.

The moral right of Andy Vassallo as the author of this work has been asserted by him in accordance with the Copyrights, Designs and Patents Act of 1988.

Published by Happy Self Publishing
www.happyselfpublishing.com

TABLE OF CONTENTS

Foreword .... *ix*
Introduction... *xiii*

1 The Current Dilemma... 1

2 The Strategy.. 7

3 Focus, Focus, Focus 25

4 Consider the Data... 39

5 Economics—The Financial Plan 51

6 Tools & Training...65

7 Alignment of the Organization 77

8 Integrate the People Systems............................. 91

9 Lead & Leverage 107

10 The Rhythm of Business 119

11 The Results... 131

Implementing the System *139*
Active Performance Execution........................*143*
Andy Vassallo Biography *145*
Acknowledgments *149*
APEX Questionnaire *151*
Thank You...*159*

FOREWORD

It is my privilege to write this Foreword for *The Focused CEO: Why Some Organizations Thrive and Others Spin Their Wheels*. I first met Andy Vassallo in 1996, which was an exciting time of great opportunity and few clear winners in the healthcare information technology field. At that time, I was Founder and CEO of a leading healthcare IT consulting company, Superior Consultant. Andy was a partner in a firm that we had a co-opetition relationship with. From the first meeting, it was obvious that Andy brought a broad view, creative thinking, and a real-world sense of how to get things done—even if perhaps others saw barriers.

Our paths crossed again several years later, when Andy was seeking a new venue to exercise his talents. After some discussion, and lengthy talks with our senior leadership, including industry leaders Charles Bracken and Rob Tashiro, Andy joined Superior to run a practice area.

Andy stood out among his peers as Superior earned meteoric growth. As you will read in *The Focused CEO*, the company faced the challenge of sustaining

Foreword

our founding principles while scaling the enterprise to a much larger business—notching 76% and 110% growth in the years following our public offering in 1996.

The second half of 1999 brought wholesale changes to our industry and to our company. Demand crashed in anticipation of Y2K. Superior's extraordinary growth leadership and managers faced a turnaround situation. New President and COO George Huntzinger, a seasoned industry veteran, came in to lead the regrouping. As Huntzinger chose his team, we agreed Andy was the person to lead our largest practice areas.

Andy's expertise in steering his part of the enterprise, along with the company's broadened service offerings, resulted in a return to profitability, and ultimately a successful upstream sale. Following the sale, Andy remained with the company and gained experience with large Fortune 500 enterprises, while I went on to found or acquire early stage businesses.

We remained in communication over the years, and when it was time to find the right person to assist with a leadership consult I was doing for a professional services enterprise, asking Andy to join me again was an easy choice. As we worked together again, I observed how much Andy had even further developed his leadership and management skills. He had begun to codify all that he had learned over the years, and as COO of that company, he steadily applied the lessons of *The Focused CEO*.

My confidence in Andy's philosophies, methods and tools of APEX management could not be more vigorously endorsed than entrusting him to apply them to a charitable cause very near and dear to my heart, "Champions of Wayne" (SM).

The Focused CEO is an easy-to-follow roadmap on how to bridge from grand goals and broad strategies to workable daily methods to achieve success. If you are facing growth challenges, profitability issues, or even disruptive market conditions, *The Focused CEO* is a must-read. Written in a conversational style, Andy Vassallo brings the characters to life in an entertaining and educational way. I suspect that many will have this book on their nightstand and as a reference source in the center of their desk as well.

If you are leading in or working in an organization that isn't realizing its potential, that just can't seem to get from the grand mission to the details of reliable execution, then *The Focused CEO* is for you. As Christopher, one of the book's primary characters, gains insight and clarity, his confidence and sense of hope grows. I believe that readers of *The Focused CEO* will experience those same feelings.

The Focused CEO is also the perfect guide for companies who are strangling progress by getting lost in the myriad of details that exist in every organization. For readers who might be feeling exhausted from long, busy days and are frustrated by a sense of failing to gain ground on major accomplishments, the book will provide relief that there is a pathway forward.

Foreword

It took a person with a Computer Scientist's attention to detail, decades of management and leadership experience, and a keen sense of the contours of today's economy, workforce and society to write this book. And that person is Andy Vassallo.

If you see the goal and want to know how to get there, then *The Focused CEO* is important. As a person who has founded, led, and guided many businesses and charitable enterprises for many decades, I can say with absolute clarity that the principles and methods put forth by Andy Vassallo work. "It works" is the strongest endorsement I can give. Hope you enjoy the read as much as I did, and that you will realize all of your greatest hopes and dreams for a bright future by applying the lessons contained.

Richard Helppie
December, 2020
Palm Desert, California

INTRODUCTION

Although there are many reasons why some businesses thrive and others struggle, in my experience, one over-arching theme that separates the extraordinary leaders from the struggling leaders lies within a focus on the details.

From Steve Jobs to John Wooden, leaders and innovators across multiple decades and from every industry have espoused the axiom "success is in the details," leaving little doubt that there is at least some truth to it. But what are these details that hold the keys to success?

I know the details that have led to years of success for myself and countless other companies. I have spent a career working with complex organizational structures and emerging companies to transform processes into efficiencies and productivity into excellence through a comprehensive business performance methodology.

This book provides leaders with the fundamentals of organizational success, detailing how to focus your team on the big ideas without losing sight of the tactical steps necessary to get there and how to develop a rhythm to continue growing stronger and more confident in the pursuit of the next great achievement.

Whether a business is a modest local operation or an enormous global conglomerate, one thing successful organizations share is a desire to grow predictively, reliably, and sustainably. That said, growth brings its own unique set of challenges:

- The organization becomes stuck, forced to spin its wheels, due to friction in the system.
- The organization is unable to continually achieve its yearly or strategic plans.
- The organization finds itself left with insufficient time to work on priority initiatives due to ongoing errors in delegation and prioritization.
- The organization has become misaligned with the company's strategy and needs to fundamentally re-group and re-focus priorities.

Sound familiar? These are just a handful of the issues I've encountered in the companies I've worked with, but this isn't a book about failures and plateaus. Instead, it's a book about organizational realignment for growth and success.

I've observed firsthand what the principles of speed, quality, and attention to detail can do for a company's success.

Details pave the way for success in organizations of all kinds, even those run by the most capable and brilliant visionaries.

Failing to address details and establish a rhythm of forward momentum means the road to positive and lasting results will be long and difficult.

What if there was a way to teach your leadership teams the process of focusing on the details and achieving the lasting results you're looking for with greater ease and efficiency?

I've spent the last three decades working side by side with various companies' management teams to embed the principles of focusing on the details. When organizations create a strong business rhythm, these principles become habit-forming, and the change process becomes organic and intuitive. This, in turn, makes the executive teams successful in the long term.

The result?

Increased profits, increased value for shareholders, rapid and sustainable growth, empowered leadership teams, and less frustrating workdays.

I've developed Active Performance Execution (APEX) as a playbook for helping your organization achieve its objectives. It's a results-driven, team-oriented method based on best practices and accountability to elicit the kind of behavioral transformation that moves mountains.

You won't find a silver bullet here or a brand selling you a lifestyle. APEX is an immersive, practical system that gets to the core of what it takes to reach your goals. To repurpose the metaphor, there's no silver bullet because we need to use an array of lead bullets.

Introduction

The APEX playbook focuses on the DETAILS with Rhythm.

We begin with developing a strategy as a vehicle to move from the current state to the desired future state. We explore concisely stating what the company does, how and why it does it, what we want to achieve, and when we want to achieve it. Then we work on focusing the whole collective organization forward to achieve stellar results.

We will discuss effectively using data with Key Performance Indicators (KPIs), dashboards, and developing predictive metrics.

We'll examine the Profit & Loss (P&L) accountability and outline the importance of knowing your cash flow, along with your return on capital, to drive predictable growth.

Then we'll dive into the tools, training, and alignment piece to ensure you're looking at the right points when it comes to providing your people with solid training, determining what tools will be the most useful for them to get the job done, and getting everyone aligned and moving forward together.

We'll look at creating integrated human systems to reinforce best practices, including, but not limited to, recruiting and hiring, orientation, performance management, and real-time, positive reinforcement in the form of recognition or compensation.

Looking at some leadership and leverage themes in terms of communicating expectations, expediting delegation, and facilitating the celebration of quality performance will also be part of our journey.

Finally, we'll discuss a business rhythm to reinforce and drive the specifics home, creating a reliable and predictable process and outcomes.

This formula wasn't thrown together overnight. Through careful cultivation (and maybe a little trial-and-error), I've compiled the most efficient ways to fit this system's methodologies together, along with the element of Rhythm. The Focused CEO provides a proven blueprint for success.

We will get into the details of the DETAILS throughout the chapters of this book. I'll break it down for you step-by-step, making it easy for you to apply the methods to your own organizations and get results.

Using a straightforward business fable narrative with real-world examples and applications to illustrate how APEX can help you:

- Create a smart culture with a strong business rhythm.
- Develop a tight strategic execution process and hit your goals.
- Build an accountable organization through better colleague development and a strong, cohesive leadership team.

At the end of the book, a series of self-assessment questions will be waiting for you to engage you in the process.

Introduction

There's nothing more satisfying than helping companies align to reach their goals. By using the APEX system and the method of focusing on the DETAILS with Rhythm, I'm confident these tried-and-true strategies will help you reach yours as well.

CHAPTER 1

THE CURRENT DILEMMA

"These are going to look great," said Kim as she forced a phone between Christopher and his computer screen.

She swiped through six photos of Christopher with his arm around a local celebrity chef. In the first set, they were in front of the chef's iconic food truck. In the second set, they were in front of Christopher's office.

"Mutual points of exposure," she said. "It's great."

"Make sure to go ahead and send him the Venmo or whatever he uses," said Christopher as he shifted his eyes from her phone to the parking lot where the food truck was loading up and back to his screen again.

"Did you even get any food?" she asked. "I heard the spicy fish taco was amazing, but I wanted to try the blackjack quesadilla. I can split my siracha bar with you," she bargained.

"I'm really not hungry," said Christopher as he shifted through a few dozen open tabs on the computer screen.

1 | The Current Dilemma

"Paid," she said, with another swipe on her phone.

Christopher's smartwatch vibrated, letting him know it was 4:45 p.m. He suffocated the alarm to turn it off. The vibration also signaled him to start paying more attention to his assistant.

"I'm always amazed you completely lose track of time after lunch on a Friday when everyone else is confirming weekend plans or scrolling through the food truck menu on their phone," she said.

Christopher gave a disenchanted nod as he moved his eyes from the screens to his desk. On the left, he had a half-read book on leadership recommended by a friend, next to a small stack of papers and envelopes—mostly bills—that had piled up over the previous weeks.

"What's the last steps?" he asked her, referring to their routine final chat of the week.

"Posting the digital pictures on social, then physical copies on the wall," she said, referencing the wall behind her. He glanced through the glass wall that made up the front of his office to a photo wall composed of celebrity guests and entrepreneurs that had stopped by to see the new company.

As Christopher looked around the office, he noticed the bulk of his staff had left for the day. Under the photo wall was an extended couch with collapsible, minimalist-desks here and there, facing a series of treadmill desks and gamer-style curved chairs that rested on the floor. To the far right, there were three other offices designated for various team leaders.

Outside the front window, the food truck cranked and pulled off through the parking lot and past the bike racks.

Just out of Christopher's sight, there was the game room packed with vintage arcade games, a Ping-Pong table, and a small, modern kitchen.

"Are you there?" joked Kim, trying to help Christopher snap out of his mental walk.

"Sorry," he said with a smile, focusing back on Kim, his chief of staff they had scooped up from Michigan State the moment she moved to town.

"Okay," she said, laying a stapled set of papers in front of her boss. "We just need approval on the new snack station. After everyone voted on Slack this week, here's the final list of items."

The young boss looked down to find a checklist of items to suit all diets. Bison jerky for the ketogenic diet fans. Non-diary peanut butter and jelly bars for the vegan bunch. Healthy chips. Non-healthy chips. A dozen types of granola snack mixes with small emoji-style images to signify which diet each item represented.

"Page two is everything to be refrigerated," she added as he flipped the page to find another set of items mostly unfamiliar to his own palate.

"I'm sure everything is fine," he said as he wondered to himself why he was still being bothered with minutia given the new product launch scheduled for next month.

She said, "I confirmed your golf game for tomorrow with the guys. I'm sure you're looking forward to that."

"It's always good to get back on the course," he said.

Kim nodded, scooped up the piece of paper from her boss's desk, and took a step toward the door. "Okay," she said. "Oh, I almost forgot. You're speaking at the middle school in a few weeks, but Jackie and I were talking, and she mentioned doing her Girls-Who-Code spiel. That way, you wouldn't really have to prepare and could sort of just follow her lead with the middle schoolers. Plus, she'll be back from vacation the day before, so you two can go over any details."

"Yeah, that sounds great. I think it's great that she wants to do that. Definitely need more quality women like yourself and Jackie in this industry."

Kim smiled and stepped out of the office. As she made her way through the front doors with her bag, the boss was finally left alone with his thoughts.

He flipped over his wrist to see 4:59 p.m. on his watch, then looked back to the screen. Looking at the open tabs, he clicked on the far left tab to begin his personal cleansing routine.

With another half dozen tabs still open, Christopher closed his laptop with a frustrated effort and disconnected the plug from the docking station. He knew it was likely to be another long night, but at least he could work from his home office.

Above the plug, he looked back to the framed photos and articles hanging on his wall. A few cherished pictures of friends and family, then a couple of photos from the launch party where he met a few of his tech heroes.

Christopher smiled, but the smile quickly evaporated when he read the headline from the article. "Will This Health Tech App Improve Your Health?" In the photo, a slightly younger version of the entrepreneur stood in front of his parents' garage, his first office.

Looking over the pile of bills and empty office, he mumbled, "Improve Your Health," to himself, shaking his head. He stuffed his laptop in his messenger bag, tossed it over his shoulder, and turned off the light of his high-dollar office.

CHAPTER 2

THE STRATEGY

- If you don't know where you are going, you'll end up someplace else.

    - Yogi Berra

- Strategy is a fancy word for coming up with a long-term plan and putting it into action.

    - Ellie Pidot

- Strategy without tactics is the slowest route to victory. Tactics without strategy is the noise before defeat.

    - Sun Tzu

"We're a player short," said a voice in Christopher's backswing.

Looking up from the practice putting green outside the Pro Shop, the young entrepreneur squinted in the morning sunlight to see his two colleagues making their way over.

Christopher looked back down, squared up his feet, and glided the putter across the green to connect with the ball. Quickly, then slowly, it rolled up to a target four feet away, then sank into the hole.

"No better sound in the world," said Terrence, the man behind the voice and Christopher's Chief Technology Officer.

"Certainly sounds better than Terrence's morning scrum call from the bullpen," joked Christopher.

Vishal, the third man on the green, smiled at the joke. "My father said the best way to gather people is to be loud about it," said the Vice President of Sales.

"A player short," said Christopher to himself, reminding the trio of their lacking foursome.

Terrence replied, "Mitch said he had to follow up with his client this morning and didn't have time to show us up on the course, or so he claimed in the text message at 5 a.m. on a Saturday morning."

The trio looked around and saw an array of golfers unpacking their clubs from vehicles, gathering to chat, and lacing up shoes, but it was difficult to tell who was together and who might be available to join their game.

"Should we just play with three?" asked Terrence.

"I was hoping to play our standard Nassau wager. I need to win my twenty-five dollars back from last week," said Christopher.

As the trio laughed together, a golf ball bounced off the back of Christopher's heel, and he turned around.

The group turned to see a man nearly thirty feet away with a putter in his hand.

"Veered left," said the man from a distance as he started to approach the group.

They looked around to see several practice holes nearby, but it was completely unclear which one the man was aiming for.

"Nice read," muttered Terrence sarcastically.

As the man drew near, the trio noticed his unusual attire. Likely in his mid-60s, he was very tan, making his spotless white polo shirt glow that much more against his skin. But, while the shirt was eye-catching, the kicker was the blue shorts with pink flamingoes on them that could've distracted an air traffic controller from two miles away.

"No stitches, I hope?" joked the man about his encounter with Christopher's foot.

"I think I'll live," responded his victim while he reached over to pick up the ball.

"Jack Ford," he said with an outstretched hand. "Call me Ford." The two men shook hands, and then

Ford repeated his name to meet Terrence and Vishal officially.

Christopher couldn't help but think that Ford looked familiar to him, at least beyond his John Daly outfit. "You here with a group?" he asked.

"No," responded Ford. "I usually come out during the week in the morning before it gets busy, but now and then I play a round on Saturday, so I thought I'd give it a go today."

Christopher eyed his colleagues for a moment to get a read but then decided to go ahead and invite Ford to play without a second opinion. "Our fourth dropped out, and we need a fourth for a friendly Nassau. Are you game?"

Ford laughed at the offer. "Well, I don't think I put my best foot forward with that first stroke, but sure, I'd love to play a round with you guys."

The newly created foursome gathered their clubs and slowly headed over to the first tee.

"Big Judge Smails fan?" joked Christopher to Ford about his opponent's wild wardrobe.

"No," he laughed, adding, "I didn't get a free bowl of soup with them," to Christopher's *Caddyshack* reference. "I love these loudmouth pants, but my wife hates them. She won't golf with me if I wear them. They remind me of Florida and my first big work assignment."

Christopher chuckled.

"But, despite that little demo you saw on the green, that was a long time ago. I am a better golfer than style guru," said Ford.

"Well, I'll give you a disclaimer as well. We are an incredibly competitive bunch, which you likely already know by our Nassau game, but I've got good days and bad days. I played a lot as a teenager, but it's rare we all get out here much anymore."

"Your boss has you burning the midnight oil, it sounds like?" asked Ford.

"I'm actually the boss," he muttered. "It's a healthcare tech startup. Vishal is our VP of sales, and Terrence is our CTO."

The two men watched as Vishal and Terrence made their way to the first tee.

"What about you?" asked Christopher.

"Oh, I'm retired," he said. "Moved down here to get warm and play golf."

"What was your line of work before you retired, if you don't mind me asking?"

"I ran a few businesses here and there," Ford replied. "I worked for a software company out of college, then a buddy and I started a company. I was a partner in another startup. I helped scale a public company during their IPO, and I've worked for a few companies in the Fortune 250."

"You've got some experience under your belt, along with those flamingoes," joked Christopher.

"I've done a little bit of everything over the years," Ford laughed. "The world has changed a lot, but at their core, companies all have similar challenges as they grow. My job was to help them maneuver through their challenges and head forward with bold intent," he said, gesturing dramatically down the green as he teed up. "Helping businesses get shit done is the technical term," he joked. "Getting unstuck or whatever it takes to move the needle, faster, through an organization. That kind of thing."

"Bold intent," Christopher repeated. "So, if I were to ask you what you think made your organizations successful, what would it be?" he asked, leaning on his club.

Ford thought for a second. "The key is to always focus on the details with rhythm. While every business is different, I have never seen a successful business not focus on the details."

Christopher's brow furrowed at the comment.

"If a company runs optimally, then it should make a point to focus on the details throughout the organization," said Ford. "Then, the action steps naturally evolve from that singular focus to match the rhythm or pulse of the organization."

"Interesting," said Christopher. "We are starting a planning session Monday to address a few current challenges. I'd be interested to hear how you planned your strategy with your teams to do those things successfully. I mean, in a nutshell."

"Well," Ford began, "Ben Hogan always said, 'The most important shot in golf is the next one.' So we are always looking forward and planning what we are going to do next, i.e., the plan. We start with a solid strategic plan that we update each year. That's fairly standard stuff. What we did that might be a little different was we had a rule that the plan must fit on one page. We felt this was one of our keys to success."

"One page? How did you manage that?"

"It can be front and back," he mused. "When done correctly, the strategic plan will provide new direction, new realities, along with vision and motivation. It will also provide resource allocation, reduce risk to the organization, and create results in a proactive organization."

"Interesting," said Christopher.

"We organize our planning meeting over two days with a group dinner to kick off the event. I have a typical agenda[1] I can share if you're interested. We would always approach the strategic planning process with the following three objectives."

The listener nodded.

---

[1] Visit www.aspensummitgroup.com/details to download a sample agenda.

Ford began, "First, you want to develop a one-page plan, then cascade the plan through the organization, and finally, make the plan stick."

"Makes sense," said Christopher.

"We get the plan done with three simple thoughts in mind. First, have a plan today. Don't wait and overthink it (i.e., exit the meeting with a plan). Second, be realistic. Climbing a mountain is easier with stairs than scaling a wall. And finally, be flexible and agile. In other words, toothpicks snap where rubber bands can flex."

Christopher thought about all his late nights, rushed projects, and weak points in his business.

"People make strategy much harder than it needs to be," Ford continued. "You can't hit your WAG in year one. That's unrealistic."

"Your WAG?" asked Christopher.

"Wild-Ass-Goal," said Ford. "A WAG is a big goal that might take ten or more years to achieve. It should also align the organization around a vision of the future with ambitious objectives."

"I see," he said.

"People want to keep analyzing and reanalyzing until their ideas are perfect, but that's overthinking it. Spend a week gathering your data, two days with the team, then roll it out. Don't let yourself get trapped in an infinite loop of analysis paralysis. Use your team. Make sure everyone knows their role in your organization, then go for it. Sometimes you need to fire first, then aim. Use your feedback to guide you, not some 1,000-page plan that wastes time and energy."

The two noticed Vishal and Terrence were gaining quick ground, so they hurried up their pace but continued the conversation.

"George Patton once said, 'A good plan, violently executed now, is better than a perfect plan next week,'" added Ford.

Christopher realized they had already reached the sixteenth hole.

"What does your current plan look like?" asked Ford. "If you don't mind me asking..."

"Not at all. Our current strategic plan fills a whole binder with all the supporting documentation. I sometimes feel like it's never read, not understood, and not embraced by the whole organization," said Christopher, shaking his head.

"That's often the case. Anything too long is often overlooked. That said, it's a lot easier than it sounds to narrow the focus," Ford said. "I always established strategy by addressing five key areas. It's all about what you can define:

- Define the purpose of the company. What outcome or result do you provide to customers?
- Define what the company does and how it does it, specifically around the company's core behaviors or values. Make it a point to spell out

what you do, how you do it, and what makes you better than the competition.
- Define the company's big rocks, that is, initiatives and goals for the year. Prioritize the rocks and break them into steps by quarter, so the rocks are achievable.
- Define the company's Key Performance Indicators (KPIs), meaning revenue targets, profit targets, number of customer targets, whatever it is within your industry that provides the right KPIs.
- Define a budget to support your plan, but don't confuse budget with strategy.

Ford continued, "Every year, we confirmed points one and two, and every quarter we'd confirm and modify as needed points three and four. How we addressed and worked out a strategic plan around these five areas changed a little depending on the different cycles of growth of the company, of course."

Christopher stepped up to the tee but kept his ears open for Ford's advice. In the pause, he stripped a bullet down the fairway.

"Big initiatives will change depending upon performance. Quarterly business reviews allowed us to keep up with those growth cycles. Then once a year, the executive team got together and conducted a two-day annual off-site meeting for strategic thinking and realignment of the plan."

"That's what we're doing this week," Christopher said with a smile while also admiring his shot. "We've been having some rough patches lately that need smoothing out, so we need to realign and come up with a strategic plan for how to address those and resolve them."

"I have worked with many brilliant people who were genius innovators and outstanding strategic thinkers," said Ford. "One time, the chief revenue officer talked a lot about defining our unfair advantage over the competition. This was hugely effective when developing strategy because when a company knows its clear strategic advantage over the competition and can perform based upon that advantage, it's poised for huge growth and market domination within its sector."

"So, after you conducted your yearly off-site meeting, how did you approach rolling out the plan to the rest of the organization?" he asked. They reached the green, and Christopher watched as Ford sank his putt.

"Before we rolled out anything at all, we had to make sure that everyone on the executive team was in complete alignment and agreement as to what our company's priority rocks were for that year, what was at the top of that list, and, most importantly, the company's defining purpose. Without that, you might as well have foregone the meeting altogether."

The group of four moved on to hole seventeen.

As they took turns teeing off, Ford looked as if he was deep in thought. "Early in my career, I worked for a company where even the owner of the company couldn't consistently communicate his company's strategic plan. He had a grand plan in his head, but it changed with a new idea every day. It was challenging for him to communicate his ideas effectively, so his ideas never resonated with the team, and they couldn't apply it to their daily jobs. He also thought everyone knew the plan as well as he did, so the lack of communication led to other problems."

At this point, Terrence and Vishal were also tuned in to the conversation.

"If the owner or CEO of an organization changes his or her mind about the company's aligning purpose and goals," said Ford, "how are the executive or key management teams supposed to deliver that owner's vision consistently? It's difficult and frustrating for everyone involved, to say the least."

"It's tempting to move toward the shiny new thing," said Christopher. "I definitely feel like I have new and good ideas daily, but that doesn't mean they're all essential for the company."

"I've met a lot of entrepreneurs who have that cat-chasing-a-laser syndrome," joked Ford. "Entrepreneurs have good ideas, which is why they're entrepreneurs, but the ability to focus on long-term goals is difficult."

Christopher nodded.

"So, we can agree that you and your team will align behind your one-page strategic plan. You'll all know forward and backward what your aligning purpose and goals are, and all of you will have the ability to communicate those clearly and effectively to the others in your organization?"

"I don't think that's unrealistic to achieve at all," said Christopher. "We have a talented team of people who believe in the company. Am I right?" he asked Vishal and Terrence.

Both men nodded their heads in agreement. "Definitely," said Vishal.

"Good," Ford exclaimed. "So, what exactly do you do?"

"It's called HealthCloud," said Christopher. "We basically transform complex data into actionable intelligence for patients, providers, and communities."

"It's everything from EMRs, to hospital records, to personal trackers, to social media and community data," added Vishal.

"That's quite a service," said Ford as he lined up his shot.

"What are your suggestions to make the plan understandable and stick with the whole organization?" asked Christopher after Ford finished his backswing.

"The next piece is not just to communicate with your team, but to make sure those messages are cascaded throughout the organization on a timely, consistent basis through multiple vehicles. It's not enough to communicate the message once during a quarterly review and then talk about it maybe in management meetings here and there."

2 | The Strategy

Christopher and his crew listened to Ford.

"Those messages—the rocks, the priorities for the company—need to be discussed every single day, every single week, every month, and at all levels of the organization, whether it be through daily stand-ups, posters in the halls, weekly email reminders, whatever. That consistent messaging will play a big part in motivating the team to succeed. Before you know it, that message starts to make its way into the rhythm of the organization. You'll see collaborations you never dreamed of as the team starts to align with the rhythm."

Christopher took a practice swing, focusing on Ford's statement.

"Another time, I worked for a CEO who was a master communicator with endless energy. His energy and information aligned the people with the objectives of the company. Back before dashboards or flat-screen TVs, his updates came in the form of a company-wide wire side chat voicemail, giving updates on the company's performance, recognizing by name key contributors, listing what our KPIs were for the day, and so on."

The trio stopped to listen to Ford.

"No one wanted to let him down, so everyone tried hard to achieve those KPIs. People wanted to be recognized company-wide in the wire side chat for kudos on a job well done, so lots of people did things above and beyond to achieve that. When people are motivated that way, extraordinary things happen for the organization."

"I can imagine," said Christopher.

"I'd be lying if I said I didn't miss it," Ford chuckled to himself. "Retirement is nice, but I miss the challenge. It was always kind of like solving a puzzle to me."

As they pulled up to the final hole, Christopher thought about himself at Ford's age. Would he feel the same way? Would his retirement be meaningful? Deep down, he was still drawn to the purpose and calling of his organization, but the day-to-day grind and ongoing hassles of running the business were no longer as rewarding as the excitement of building a small team when he first began his company.

Ford studied Christopher's expression. He could see he was deep in thought. "Just make sure your strategic plan is concise, clear, simple, and well-constructed, so when you get back, your management teams don't have to dig around to find the unifying plan. Nothing's worse than when a plan is so obtuse and complicated that your key managers don't even want to look at it, much less take the time they don't have to interpret and translate it. Complexity stops progress."

"Good advice!" joked Terrence from across the green.

Ford added, "When everyone knows what the goals are, everyone sees how it's going to get done, how they're going to do it, and knows what the company's big purpose is, real magic can happen within the organization to achieve your goals."

Ford patted Christopher on the back. He felt some relief as the foursome finished up their round.

"We'll see you for dinner," said Terrence as the two walked to their car.

Christopher waved as his colleagues made their way to the parking lot. "You mentioned the details," he said to Ford. "I'm not entirely sure I know what you mean specifically. Could I buy you lunch and have you tell me a little more about this system you've established? I know you're retired and all. If you don't feel like talking shop, I get it."

"I'm always up for lunch," joked Ford, "And I'm always up for talking shop."

"What's your method called, anyway?" asked Christopher.

"As Peter Drucker says, 'Strategy is a commodity, execution is an art.' The secret sauce is the ability to execute the strategy. That's why I refer to the process as Active Performance Execution, or APEX for short," said Ford.

The Focused CEO

Later that night, Christopher pulled out his notebook and recorded his notes on Strategy based on his conversation with Ford.

STRATEGY NOTES

1. Utilize a One-Page Strategy document.
   - Don't overthink your strategy—take action!
   - Keep it real on your climb—don't try to reach your WAG in one year
   - Include the people in your decisions and strategy sessions

2. Cascade strategic initiatives throughout the organization.
   - Everyone should know their role in the company's objectives
   - Everyone should know their team's role in the company
   - Everyone should know who to contact for questions or specifics

3. Make the plan stick by establishing...
   - Everyone can articulate the company's big rocks
   - Everyone understands the brand's promises
   - Everyone understands the 90-second pitch

Make sure to visit the back of the book to take the self-assessment and visit www.aspensummitgroup.com/details to download the free companion workbook or schedule a one-on-one with Andy Vassallo.

CHAPTER 3

FOCUS, FOCUS, FOCUS

- You will never reach your destination if you stop and throw stones at every dog that barks.
    - Winston Churchill

- Concentrate all your thoughts upon the work at hand. The sun's rays do not burn until brought to a focus.
    - Alexander Graham Bell

- The successful warrior is the average man, with laser-like focus.
    - Bruce Lee

"My assistant recommended this place," said Christopher as he reached out to shake hands with Ford. "She recommends—"

"The huevos rancheros?" asked Ford.

3 | Focus, Focus, Focus

"Yes, actually," smiled Christopher. "How did you—"

"The usual, Ford?" asked a friendly hostess who placed her hand on Ford's back and started to escort the duo toward an open table.

"Two," replied the regular. "Much appreciated."

The duo sat down, and Christopher looked Ford over again, once again surprised by this new acquaintance.

"Tell me a little about your business and what challenges you're facing right now."

"As you might remember, we're a mid-sized tech company," Christopher began, not wasting any time. "We combine data from multiple healthcare sources such as Physician EMRs, hospital data, claims data, personal trackers, social media, environmental, and community information to produce futuristic predictions of a patient's health. This helps people with chronic illnesses."

"I remember," replied Ford.

"Our first five years were record-breaking, which is great. We had tremendous growth. But the last two years have had up-and-down revenue with flat EBITDA (Earnings Before Interest, Taxes, Depreciation, and Amortization). Now we're rolling out this new product, and things are moving so fast it has kind of derailed us a little bit in a couple of areas."

Ford shook out the silverware and tossed a napkin in his lap.

"What's at the forefront of my mind right now are some of the bumps in the road we've been having with efficiency and delivery. Particularly, we have a tough time keeping our engineers busy. It's gotten me into a situation where there's concern within the team, and it's cutting into our profit. As you can imagine, it's affecting everyone. It's come to the point that I'm looking at our sales manager to pull us out of this slide."

Ford was quiet. He looked like he was searching for something to say. The waitress dropped off two glasses of water and two drinks in highball glasses with watermelon slices on the rim.

"Don't worry—just a watermelon mocktail," joked Ford.

Christopher smiled at the unusual usual.

"After creating and updating a strategy to ensure it's not shelfware, you need to execute the strategy. The first step is to create organizational Focus," said Ford. "Alexander Graham Bell once said, 'Concentrate all your thoughts upon the work at hand. The sun's rays do not burn until brought to a focus.' Have you heard that one?"

"No but I get the gist of what he's trying to communicate."

"Well, let's start with the sun then," said Ford. "Did you know that every hour, the sun hits the earth with over 430 quintillion joules of energy?"

Christopher smiled, sipping his mocktail. "I did not."

"Well, 430 quintillion is 430 with eighteen zeroes after it. Hard to wrap your head around, isn't it? The thing is, we don't really notice it. The sun's enormous power gets fanned out in all directions, and when it reaches earth, it's enough to keep us warm and sustain life, but it doesn't necessarily perform a focused task. If you take that energy and focus it, say through a magnifying glass or solar panel, that energy becomes concentrated and can be used to do all kinds of things, from starting a fire to powering a home."

"Right."

"A similar concept applies to low-power devices such as flashlights or lasers. When you focus that low power through a laser lens, you get concentrated energy. That energy can accomplish remarkable things like eye surgery and precision cutting. It can even cut through the densest materials on earth using only a minuscule fraction of a fraction of the level of energy that the sun puts out."

"I see where you're going with this..." said Christopher. "Take twenty steps in one direction rather than one step in twenty directions."

"Yes, and that applies to everyone, not just you and your leaders. One or two people can achieve short-term growth, but consistent growth in an organization requires the whole organization's forward movement to achieve their goal. It requires focus from everyone involved. If that energy gets harnessed, it will do great things."

Christopher nodded.

"Have you heard the story of Charles Schwab and Ivy Lee?" Ford asked.

"I know who Charles Schwab is. I mean, I use them for my investments, but I've never heard of Ivy Lee," said Christopher.

"Not Charles Schwab of Wall Street. I'm talking about Charles M. Schwab. He was the CEO of Bethlehem Steel, the second largest steelmaker in the U.S. in its day."

"When was 'its day'?" asked Christopher.

"At the turn of the last century on up through 2003," joked Ford. "Back in the late 1800s, Ivy Lee was a management consultant who worked with titans like Rockefeller and Carnegie. He also consulted with Schwab. When they met, Schwab informed him that he didn't need someone to teach him his business. He needed someone to show him a faster way to get the things done he already knew how to do."

Just then, the waitress dropped off two hot sizzling meals consisting of perfectly poached eggs over warm tortillas, with crumbled feta cheese, cilantro, black beans, hot sauce, and an array of onions, jalapeños, and garlic.

"Wow, this looks great," said Chris.

"Thank you," replied Ford to the waitress. Looking back to Christopher, he continued, "So the story goes, Lee asked Schwab to write down the three most important things he needed to get done that day and prioritize them. He told Schwab to keep the list with him, start at the top, and work on that one item until it was done. Only when it was done should he then move on to the next item on the list, and so on. Schwab adopted that habit of focus, and the rest is history as they say."

"So, what ended up happening to Ivy Lee?" asked Christopher.

"Well, he spent a few minutes giving Schwab some advice and got paid $25,000 for it," said Ford.

"What? I don't even know the conversion rate from then to now, but that was a serious boatload of money for back then."

"It certainly was," said Ford. "But nothing compared to what he made from the advice. He told Schwab to pay him what he thought the advice was worth, and apparently, it had been *that* beneficial. It provided Schwab with a quick and easy way to get things done. It showed him how to focus."

"Are you saying these huevos rancheros are going to cost me $25,000?" joked Christopher.

Ford laughed. "No, nothing like that. The real point is that this isn't an old-fashioned idea that got stuck back in the 1900s. It's still applicable to best practices today." Ford tapped on the table. "So, you do it. Write down the three most important items you need to do tomorrow."

"Now?" asked Christopher.

"Now," Ford reiterated.

Christopher waved down the server to borrow a pen and a piece of paper, and he wrote out the three most important things he had to do tomorrow.

"Ok, if you've got them, work on item number one and say 'No' to everything else until it's finished. Then the same with number two. Say 'No' to everything but the item you're working on until you graduate to the next. Try this every day for a few days, and I guarantee you'll be more focused and get more done in a shorter amount of time. Your willpower to eliminate the non-essentials will also grow as you become confident within the system."

The server came to the table with a second round of drinks already made, but this time she had prepared two Arnold Palmers for the table.

"How often do you come here?" asked the newcomer.

"Concentration comes from a combination of confidence and hunger." He looked at Christopher and smiled. "Arnold Palmer said that. Resist the urge to create an action plan with a million action items. Instead, focus them on the top three to five—three is better—that need to be addressed ASAP to start you on the path you want. Make sure you identify the most important item."

3 | Focus, Focus, Focus

Christopher sipped the new drink.

"You exerted a lot of energy, that's for sure, but you need to harness the power of the whole organization. I worked with a healthcare tech company that was having similar issues as yours," he continued. "They were struggling with the utilization rate of their staff. Profits were sinking, and no one was hitting their bonuses. We were even looking at potential layoffs. We instituted a program for every group in the organization, not just management and team leaders, to focus on the single goal of putting all the analysts on projects."

"That makes sense," said Christopher.

"First, we let everyone know we had an issue, the ramifications of the situation, and enlisted their help in finding a solution. We let them know that we had to find more projects, but we wanted everyone's help—not just the sales team."

The listener took another big bite.

"We focused them on the single most important issue, made it urgent, then ramped up the energy of the company behind it. We held one daily call with everyone in the process—sales, delivery, HR, and finance teams—with the sole purpose of tracking progress and eliminating roadblocks to new projects."

Christopher pushed his finished plate to the side.

"We reviewed the current utilization rates of the analysts and focused on action points to implement *that day.* Not every week, but daily. When we started the program, the colleagues reported that they were going to call customers or work on a proposal, but that's too broad. We required them to submit a more focused, detailed accountability status that included which customers they were contacting, why they were calling them, and the expected outcome of the calls."

"Wow. I'm sure everyone looked forward to *those* meetings every day!" Christopher laughed.

Ford chuckled, "Oh, they hated them! But after we implemented the daily accountability, you should have heard the conversations around the company. Every person was talking about the specific things—the details—of what they were doing that day."

Christopher felt like a light was going on. "So narrowing the focus meant that the organization became aligned?"

"To a degree, yes. Let me give you an example from the sales team. The sales reps would provide an update on their planned actions. Notice the difference between these two status updates."

Salesperson One: "I'm going to call my customers, follow up on the leads from the billing seminar, and work on a proposal."

OR

Salesperson Two: "I'm going to call Mr. Smith, the CIO at St. Mary's hospital, regarding their planned EMR purchase, and call Ms. Watson, the CFO at General

Hospital, regarding her project to improve denied claims. We received 123 leads from our line-billing seminar, and I'll sort the list by those with the largest reported Medicare population and call the top ten. I will focus on calling the CFOs but will also call the CEOs. I'll ask Jane, my CFO, for ten minutes of her help because St. Hope wants to modify the payment terms of their proposal."

"I see, definitely different," Christopher mused.

"Specific, not general," he said. "Statement two provides much greater insight and detail. It also holds the person reporting accountable for knowing their focus for the day and reporting back their success or failure," said Ford. "The focus was on moving things forward to closing—not just on keeping busy. You can be highly efficient at things that don't matter."

"Of course."

"The next day, we reviewed those detailed action steps. Did they make the calls? Who did they talk to? Did they get the outcome they expected? If not, what was the outcome? What roadblocks can we remove? Then we brainstormed ideas and suggestions for the winning strategy."

"That makes sense."

"We also started keeping a focused daily scorecard to accompany these action steps. If the sales team closed a sale, they won for the day. If not, they lost. We looked at the daily win rates and connected them to the whole week to look for patterns of accountability and execution."

Christopher sipped his drink.

"As you can imagine, these calls were very intense because they required everyone to discuss in detail their performance and planned action steps. It became easy to pinpoint who was working on their plan daily and who wasn't. Everyone was held accountable for their daily activities. 'What gets measured gets managed' as Peter Drucker has said."

The waitress stopped by to remove an unused dish.

Ford continued, "Now, some would say that this was too much, and we micromanaged everyone to death. Others may think of it as good, sound management reviews. Either way, it focused the *whole* team—sales, operations, and corporate support teams—on what was important. We never told people what to do or how to do it. We focused them on outcomes, provided direction, and removed roadblocks if they got stuck."

"How did it turn out?" asked Christopher. "Did you get the results you wanted in the time you wanted them?"

"We did," Ford exclaimed. "Everyone became aligned and focused on the most important goal for the quarter. Once we got everyone executing those smaller steps and moving in the same direction, we got big results. We turned the issues around in two months, became profitable again, and everyone received their bonuses."

Christopher raised his eyebrows and leaned back in his chair. "Did everyone stay on track *after* that?"

"They did—for two reasons," said Ford. "One, because they learned to prioritize what's important and how to take focused, actionable steps to work on that *every day*. Two, because the program did not end. This was not some onetime action. We continued with a workable meeting and reporting rhythm. Six months after the focused program, I got feedback from multiple people that it was hugely beneficial for them, and they saw measurable improvements in their metrics and personal achievements."

"Wow," said Christopher, intently thinking how to apply the rules to his own team. Then his watch vibrated, letting him know he needed to head back to work.

Ford reached for his wallet. "I've got to get back soon too," he said.

"Oh no, you don't!" said Christopher. "Lunch is on me, remember? It's been really interesting."

The men exchanged business cards. "Don't be too shy to give me a shout if you need to," said Ford. "I'm happy to help."

"I may do that," laughed Christopher. "Is there more to your system?"

"There is," said Ford.

"I'll tell you what," said Christopher. "Would you want to meet me for a round at our usual spot at home next

Saturday and continue our conversation about your method? It's on me."

"That sounds great!" said Ford.

"Great. I'll make a tee time and give you a call next week."

On his way back to the office, Christopher thought about the things they had talked about. Was a lack of focus his problem? He didn't think so, but then again, it wouldn't hurt to revisit the idea with his team and work through the exercises Ford laid out for him. They decided to put it on the agenda for when they got back to the office.

3 | Focus, Focus, Focus

That afternoon, Christopher pulled out his notebook and recorded his notes on Focus based on his conversation with Ford.

FOCUS NOTES

1. Focus the sun's power for maximum results and leverage.
   - Create a sense of urgency
   - Involve the whole team
   - Focus your lens on the most important item to accomplish

2. Use a Daily Top-3 to help prioritize schedules and focus.
   - Don't prioritize your schedule, only schedule priorities
   - Say "NO" to non-priorities (or at least, "not now")
   - Encourage other leaders in your company to do the same

3. Get into the details of accountability to maximize results.
   - Understand how to track daily points of accountability
   - Focus on specific actionable and measurable tasks
   - Gather failures as well as successes to understand results

Make sure to visit the back of the book to take the self-assessment and visit www.aspensummitgroup.com/details to download the free companion workbook.

CHAPTER 4

CONSIDER THE DATA

- Without data, you're just another person with an opinion.
    - **- Edward Deming**

- Errors using inadequate data are much less than those using no data at all.
    - **- Charles Babbage**

- There's no such thing as bad weather, only unsuitable clothing.
    - **- Alfred Wainwright**

Over the next week, the strategy planning sessions with Christopher's team went by quickly. When he returned to the office, the young CEO started using Ford's tips on focus. Each day, he found himself getting into the habit of writing the three most important tasks he needed to complete every morning and working through them. When the weekend rolled around, Christopher met up with Ford at their hometown course.

"So, tell me how it went last week?" asked Ford after a few friendly pleasantries. "Did you find the suggestions about focus and strategy we talked about helpful?"

"I did," said Christopher. "It's been helpful. I even passed the advice on to the team."

"Good," said Ford. "That's often the hard part. Suggestions are one thing, but implementation and accountability are key to any real type of success."

"What's the next step?" Christopher asked as he stepped up to the green on the first hole.

Ford took his putt and missed just left, then tapped it in for bogie. "Now that you have your strategy set and are focused, you need to achieve your plan. When you successfully execute your plan, you generate more growth, more profit, and have more fun at work. Having fun while growing with healthy profits is the perfect trifecta."

Chris faced Ford to listen closer.

"The next phase of executing your plan is creating active performance excellence, or APEX, in multiple areas of the organization. Some might refer to this as operational efficiency. I like to add the word 'active' because it requires focused activity every day in all areas of the organization."

The duo walked toward the next tee.

Ford said, "Let's start with what data you use."

"I was having a conversation about data reporting with Vishal last week," said Christopher. "You remember Vishal?"

"Yes," said Ford. "VP of sales?"

"That's right. You've got a good memory."

"Thanks," Ford smiled. "I work on it."

"Hit me with your advice on data usage," said Christopher.

"Let's start with the *why* first," Ford began. "Using data to drive decisions and workflows will result in increased accountability, transparency, and an improved feedback loop. Improvement in these areas will then drive the organization to be more aware, proactive, responsive, and confident."

Christopher squinted in the sunlight to see Ford's face.

"The final benefit is my favorite, and that is creating an organization that will explore the *why*. Exploring the *why* results in new patterns being observed and increases the number of new questions asked. These new questions drive an increased desire for more data and using data to make more informed decisions."

The two continued across the green.

"I suggest starting with the use of scorecards and dashboards of key performance indicators (KPIs).

At a minimum, each dashboard should include the item reported, the current value, the target value, and the change in value since the last report. Some organizations will report more, but start with these items, if you are new to dashboards."

"I agree. We use dashboards in various areas now," said Christopher.

"All departments and groups within the organization should create a dashboard. Using a dashboard in only one or two areas is risky, plus it makes them seem like a fad, solution of the month, or somehow punitive to those groups using them."

"I've noticed similar issues with our current data," said Christopher.

"Everyone likes to play on a winning team," said Ford, "and every person wants to know how they are contributing to the win."

Christopher nodded.

Ford continued, "So start at the top. What are the three 'must-wins' for the company? That's your first dashboard measure. Now, go to sales. How do they help meet those goals? That becomes their top three, and so on."

"Right," said Christopher.

"You can start with one or two groups, but make sure you have a plan to roll out all areas and make sure everyone knows the plan. It is more important to start using a dashboard tomorrow than wait months while the perfect KPI is determined. Good dashboards will spur new creativity, which inspires communication across teams. It is the improved decisions that result from this dialogue that drives the increased productivity."

"That makes sense," said Christopher.

"The dashboards should be publicly displayed for all to see, and data needs to be a natural byproduct of the workflow. The information also needs to be updated and discussed daily. Posting publicly creates awareness and importance and prevents data silos from forming. You will know you are on the right track when the team discusses how to provide a KPI before leadership."

"So, where should we start? What should we measure?"

Ford answered, "First, let's start with the definition of a KPI. A KPI is a business metric that shows how effective an organization is in achieving its goals. It can be financial or non-financial, but it needs to be measurable. The exact KPIs on a dashboard will be driven by the department, team, industry, and organization's goals. I recommend each organization look at their current situation and goals when developing their initial set of KPIs."

"How does that play into predictive measures?" asked Christopher.

"Great question. When organizations only have historical KPIs, it is kind of like driving and only looking in the rearview minor. Historic KPIs tell you what has happened, but it's virtually important to have predictive KPIs. The predictive KPIs are KPIs that happen at various times prior to the key historical KPIs. You still want historical data, but you use it to predict the future."

"So, let's say the goal is to double revenue. What do we measure?" asked Christopher.

"Right," said Ford. "So, in this example, let's say last year we did $1 million in revenue and this year we want to do $2 million. Let say that at the end of the quarter, we did $700,000 of revenue versus a target of $500,000. Management might conclude that we are on track to hit the year-end target of $2 million and that they could expect to exceed it."

"Sure," said Christopher. "Hypothetically, that makes sense."

"Now let's say we also had KPIs that showed orders placed for next quarter, or a KPI that showed availability of widgets to build our product. If either of these metrics caused a critical shortage, leadership would see a potential problem before it occurred."

"Like a department store ordering 10,000 swim trunks in September—at the end of swim season," confirmed Christopher.

"Exactly. This would also tell the organization to put into place alternative plans to make up a shortage or create more orders. Now while this oversimplified example may not be true, it shows the importance of KPIs that can possibly predict future performance."

Christopher nodded, thinking back on his own business.

"With predictive KPIs, an organization can significantly increase their odds of hitting their strategic objectives. The third leg of data usage is using the rule of three when analyzing the data for insights. The rule of three is like asking why something is happening, answering the why, and doing that three times in a row."

Ford explained:
- On a whiteboard, write down an import business metric (it can be any metric).
- Write "WHY?" next to it.
- Brainstorm the most likely reasons the metric occurred. Write these reasons on the whiteboard.
- Next to each reason, *estimate* the impact to the bottom line if you fixed/improved that item (don't worry about qualifying the amounts exactly, as I've seen groups get frozen trying to quantify these items for months).
    o For the item with the largest impact, ask yourself, "Why does this occur?"
    o Brainstorm the most likely reasons the metric occurred. Write these reasons on the whiteboard.
    o Next to each one, *estimate* the impact to the bottom line if you fixed/improved that item.
        ▪ For the item with the largest impact,

ask yourself, "Why does this occur?" for the third time.
- Brainstorm the most likely reasons the metric occurred.
- Next to each one, *estimate* the impact to the bottom line if you fixed/improved that item.

- Then, congratulate yourself because you've found the most important thing to work on.
- Now, spend 80 percent of your time solving/improving this item before moving on.

Ford added, "It's similar to the daily tasks for individuals, but focused on the larger group."

Christopher smiled at the elegant solution.

"But that's just the beginning. With every member of your team and however you break up your teams, you need to understand how to implement the data. Like our weekly sessions out here, you need scorecards, dashboards, and KPIs to improve your game. But in your business, you need to publicly post the data, update the data, and use it regularly. There's nothing worse than a team who feels like they're doing busywork that they don't see implemented."

"I've worked with those types of companies. Frustrating, to say the least," he responded.

"And, of course, don't use the data in the wrong way. Never spin the data. Don't justify what you're already doing, but evaluate what you're doing to make it better.

The Focused CEO

See the true value of your data, and it will change everything. This also takes some of the pressure off your company. Everything is an experiment to collect data, not just a pass-fail race to stay the same or justify wasteful habits."

Christopher thought about an earlier conversation he had with Vishal the previous week. During their chat, Vishal discussed a sales pipeline, leads, quotes, wins, and losses, but beyond the briefing, they did little with the data.

"As I said, take inventory of the data you have available to you so that you can evaluate how to use that data to make smarter decisions. You should have data on the following four key pillars of your organization: the financials, your customers, your colleagues, and your internal processes."

Christopher thought about his company and what type of data they collected.

"Then, categorize that data by whether it's result-driven, process-driven, or predictive. Next, write down what answers you wish you had. Not the questions, but the actual answers you want. Determine what data you need to answer these questions and start collecting it as soon as possible."

Christopher wiped the sweat from his brow. As Ford continued, he started to list potential ideas of how to collect better data from his team and how to condense Ford's message so each team member would better understand how to collect data and what types of data to collect.

As if he were reading Christopher's mind, Ford concluded: "Then, as you reach out to your team members, ask them a few simple questions. Does every team member have valuable KPI? How can you best present daily scorecards to measure growth? How can data move the needle to improve decisions and ongoing processes in your organization?"

Listening intently, Christopher thought deeply about the questions and even got excited to share these new ideas with his team on Monday.

The Focused CEO

After the game, Christopher pulled out his notebook and recorded his notes on Data based on his conversation with Ford.

DATA NOTES

1. Use scorecards/dashboards/KPIs for all teams.
   - Publicly post results
   - Update data charts/results daily
   - Avoid confusion and distraction of the team with "solution of the month"

2. KPIs need to include predictive data points, not just reactive data points.
   - Use charts and graphs to analyze data whenever possible
   - Analyze monthly, quarterly, and annual tends
   - Predictive metrics should include behavior-based activities

3. Use the "Rule of 3" to drill into your data.
   - When exploring the data, ask "why" at least 3 times
   - When you have an answer, ask "why" again
   - When you have this answer, ask "why" again

Make sure to visit the back of the book to take the self-assessment and visit www.aspensummitgroup.com/details to download the free companion workbook or schedule a one-on-one with Andy Vassallo.

CHAPTER 5

ECONOMICS—THE FINANCIAL PLAN

- Beware of little expenses; a small leak will sink a great ship.
  - Benjamin Franklin

- You don't know what pressure is until you play for five bucks with only two bucks in your pocket.
  - Lee Trevino

- We were always focused on our profit and loss statement. But cash flow was not a regularly discussed topic. It was as if we were driving along, watching only the speedometer, when in fact we were running out of gas.
  - Michael Dell

Following his meeting with Ford, Christopher returned to work and began implementing the best practices on data they had discussed. He was amazed

5 | Economics—The Financial Plan

at how quickly the rest of the team picked up on and utilized the lessons with their own teams. One day after work, he came home to a note waiting for him on the kitchen counter: *Meet me at Jen's house.*

Christopher went upstairs to change out of his work clothes and then walked over to their neighbors' house. Jen had been their neighbor for years and had been a godsend to Christopher and his wife. When they were younger, she was always up for watching the kids for much-needed date nights now and then, and the kids loved her. Win-win.

When he knocked on the back door, he could see Jen and his wife having coffee at the kitchen table. Jen waved him in. The smell that hit him when he opened the door made his mouth water.

"Hey!" she said. "You're just in time for my experimental cookie recipe."

They talked for a little while about day-to-day stuff, and Christopher asked how business was going. Jen had owned a successful, well-established local staffing company for about 20 years, with about 130 employees.

She had been talking about selling and retiring within the year. They discussed how she was ready to go through the process of getting the company positioned to sell. The last few years had slower growth than expected, and margins took a hit, so she was working on a plan to position the company for maximum value.

Jen joked that when the time came to sell, she was going to tap Christopher's contacts within the venture capital word.

Christopher said he would be happy to help. He remembered when he was raising money for HealthTech, various contacts really helped out, and now was the time to pay it forward.

The next day, Christopher and Ford met for their weekly match. The duo met up at their usual spot that Saturday morning, hit a bucket of balls, then began their round. They caught up and talked about work, friends, and family for a while.

"So, you said you'd tell me about the next step of your system," said Christopher. "What's next?"

"Remember, these are items within the business that you need to focus on to achieve your strategic goals. They are not steps that need to happen in any order to be successful. They can be worked in parallel and at various speeds."

"Right," said Christopher as he practiced his swing.

"All that being said, the next thing we should review is making sure the company has a sound economic foundation. Corporate financials are a complex topic, and people get degrees in finance, accounting, economics, etc. I'm not a CFO, but what I do know is every company needs a solid, rock hard financial foundation to build on. I suggest you get the following three items tight, and the rest will follow:

- Understand cash is king.
- Understand Profit and Loss (P&L) accountability.
- Understand steady growth principles."

"This is my kind of topic. I love cash," joked Christopher. "Oh, and just in case you forgot, I am up ten dollars in our match."

"Consider yourself pressed," Ford laughed. "I have not forgotten; I get candy on the next two holes."

"Done," said Christopher.

"It's essential that you know what drives your company from an economic standpoint. Profit, revenue streams, expenses, and cash flow, for instance."

Christopher nodded along as they walked the course.

"John Mullins said, 'Revenue is vanity; profit is sanity; cash flow is reality.' Additionally, countless others have used the phrase 'cash is king.' The point is that cash is the most important and is the real currency," Ford said with air quotes. "Until revenue and profit are converted to cash, they cannot be used to make payroll."

"That makes sense," said Christopher.

"I've always said, 'I'd rather win five dollars and play lousy golf than lose five dollars and play well, but if I can play well and win five dollars, the drinks taste that much better.'"

"Cash is king," reiterated the protégé.

"Everyone has heard that cash is king, but why do so many companies just run out of cash?" Ford asked. "Do you know how to make sure your company systems and culture generate cash? When we look at a company's financial plan, we begin by assessing cash on hand. We determine how many months' worth of cash they need and how they could potentially adjust cash flow levers."

Christopher listened, thinking about his own cash flow.

"Personally, I've managed through three or four economic downturns, and having cash on hand allows you to sustain those downtimes as well as invest in the business to emerge stronger than your competitors when the economy *does* turn around. More cash allows for more investment in research and development or sales staffing. With a strong balance sheet, it also allows you to scale quickly."

"How much cash on hand did you keep as a rule? I've seen suggestions all over the place from three months to one year," asked Christopher.

"I've seen some materials recommend keeping three months of cash on hand, but we always planned for six to twelve months to be on the conservative side. I find that a nice cash base results in more confidence and security. With confidence, you can make more rational decisions. Outstanding cash flow is like fuel for your

5 | Economics—The Financial Plan

business, allowing you to fund growth-producing activities."

"That makes sense," said Christopher.

"Understanding your cash flow levers in your business is of utmost importance. When you understand the levers and their effects on your business, you can optimize them for any situation. In general, these are the key areas that affect cash flow," said Ford. "And you need to make sure they're reviewed frequently to ensure you're maximizing cash flow into the company, such as:

1. Price
2. Volume
3. Expenses
4. Collection pace or accounts receivable
5. Cost of inventory

"In addition to these tractional cash flow levers, it is important to look at how you can interact with your customers to increase cash flow," said Ford.

Christopher took another practice swing while listening to Ford.

"For example, upfront collections, invoicing at the beginning of the month versus the end of the month, having subscription-based sales, and evergreen contracts that automatically renew so that your cost of sale goes down (and once somebody signs up, the likelihood of staying is increased). There's looking at the frequency of your transactions, increasing your transaction size, and looking for add-on sales or your expansion opportunities."

"Right."

"We used to have a saying in a company I worked for," said Ford. "You're always trying to find the next Barbie doll. Meaning, if you think about the Barbie doll, she'd retail for ten or fifteen dollars. But what really made money for the company was that a parent might buy a ten-dollar Barbie and then spend $300 over the next couple of years for accessories."

"The customer journey," clarified Christopher.

"Clothes, car, house, friends, and so on. So, while you have that cost in sale to get them to purchase, or invest in, the original product, make sure they stick around and buy additional services, like radiating your products and services within that customer base."

"Another great analogy."

"My third recommendation when creating a financial plan," Ford continued, "is to plan for reality, then overachieve. It's important to set yourself up for success by aiming for predictable, constant improvement rather than jumping to reach what I call the magical benchmark. I've seen plenty of companies rely on hockey stick forecasts to get where they need to be, only to fail to get there."

"I agree about how unrealistic hockey stick forecasts are—I have never seen them work," commented Christopher. "Our application coders like to refer to the FM button as a way to get a project back on track. I guarantee that we are aware of the dangers of relying on magic."

Ford responded, "Vince Lombardi once said, 'Hope is not a strategy.' That's why I'd rather see predictable, incremental improvements every step of the way. Companies can also get hung up on industry benchmarks and metrics when forecasting performance. Maybe they're at a 20 percent margin, but the industry benchmark may be 45 percent. It's easy to get all caught up in how to get to 45 percent, but, depending on the stage of growth or product maturity, it's just not realistic to assume you'll get there as fast as you'd like."

"I've been there," replied Christopher.

"Or consider a situation where the struggle to hit that 45 percent benchmark requires cuts or changes in the business that the organization isn't prepared to make. That's why steady, incremental progress will get you there much faster than relying on magical hockey stick forecasts that may cost the company money anyway or demotivate your team if they can't reach their goals. I'd also suggest implementing an accountability P&L matrix. A lot of organizations assume the responsibility for the P&L rests solely with the CFO," said Ford as he chipped his ball up onto the green, just missing the cup and stopping a foot past the hole.

"Aww, so close!" Christopher said to his opponent.

"Don't get me wrong, the CFO and their team generate the P&Ls and are deeply involved," he continued as he finished the putt. "But what a P&L matrix does is create multiple views and accountabilities. When accountability is distributed, you get a multiplication of the focus. So instead of one person focused on something, you get two or three sets of eyes."

Christopher finished the hole just under par.

"Nice," said Ford. "For each line of the corporate P&L, someone was accountable, and additionally, each functional area of the company had a P&L. This means creating vertical and horizontal interactions of accountability and focus. So, you'll need both primary and secondary accountability for all areas of the P&L. You want to aim for maximum value within each line. It's not only about reducing costs for cost items but also about maximizing value."

"Maximizing value," Christopher repeated to himself.

"For example, if we want to improve our customer experience and net promoter scores, we can create an accountability matrix across multiple planes. So, the VPs of each region were responsible for scores in their region. The VP of product design was responsible across their products, and the VP of support was also responsible. Three views. Multiple teams working collaboratively for the same objective. This increased communications and data sharing and reduced the chance of people looking the other way on customer issues."

5 | Economics—The Financial Plan

Christopher nodded.

"In the sales functions, we did the same thing. The VP of sales was responsible for review across the company. The VP of each product was responsible for their products' revenue, and the field engineers were responsible for revenue in their regions. This helped to control and manage working together to reduce those costs and maximize revenue."

On the following hole, Christopher tapped in for bogie.

"You might be surprised at how many companies forget to stop and put enough focus on those three areas. It makes a significant difference if you'd like to see consistent yet rapid improvement."

Christopher marked his score. It was better than he'd played in a while. "I think these weekly meetings are good for my game," he laughed.

"I do too," said Ford. "Nice shot."

As the men walked back to the Pro Shop, Ford brought up a final point. "You know, the piece on accounting and finance comes up frequently during times of economic downturn, or when a CEO or business owner is preparing to sell. There is not a magic bullet or one thing that gets a company back on track financially, but being fiscally responsible is a process, and keeping an eye on your cash is an everyday thing."

The listener turned to face Ford.

"All of these points help create a predictable, steady improvement with your cash, so you don't overcommit in any given area. As the saying goes, it's easier to reach the summit when you stop at basecamp."

Christopher bought the duo both a drink from the vending machine.

"Much obliged." Ford said, "When someone purchases a company, they want to know that the organization is a solid, dependable cash producing machine. They don't want to see onetime financial maneuvers that made the company profitable and successful."

"Love it. This is useful advice that I can incorporate into my company and share with a friend of mine hoping to sell her business. I'll be looking into that P&L matrix when I get back on Monday too," said Christopher.

They posted their scores and walked to their cars.

"So, are you free next week for Saturday golf?" he asked.

"Sure. Same time?" Ford asked, loading his clubs into his trunk.

"Yep. My treat. I'd like to hear more," Christopher laughed. "If you feel like sharing, that is."

"Always," Ford laughed. "See you next Saturday!"

Before he left the parking lot, Christopher pulled out his notebook and recorded his notes on Economics based on his conversation with Ford.

ECONOMICS NOTES

1. Have a cash reserve of at least six (6) months. Twelve (12) is best.

2. Know and Understand your cash flow levers. Such as the following:
   - Price
   - Volume
   - Expenses
   - Indirect/direct and overhead expenses
   - Collection pace or accounts receivable
   - Cost of inventory

3. Know and understand what other items impact cash flow? Such as the following:
   - Upfront collections
   - Invoicing at the beginning of the month vs. the end of the month
   - Having subscription-based sales and evergreen contracts that automatically renew so that your cost of sale goes down, and once somebody signs up, the likelihood of staying is increased.
   - Looking at the frequency of your transactions, increasing your transaction size.
   - Also looking for add-on sales or your expansion opportunities.

4. Create a Profit & Loss accountability matrix.
   - Creates multiple views of responsibility
   - Creates multiple points of accountability
   - Creates multiple points of focus
5. Create a Culture of predictable, steady improvement.
   - Don't overcommit
   - Focus on steady growth
   - Easier to reach the summit when stopping to camp at basecamps along the way

CHAPTER 6

TOOLS & TRAINING

- Technology is nothing. What's important is that you have faith in people, that they're basically good and smart, and if you give them tools, they'll do wonderful things with them.

  - Steve Jobs

- I never lose. I either win, or I learn.

  - Nelson Mandela

- Every day that I missed practicing takes me one day longer to be good.

  - Ben Hogan

As Saturday drew near, it became evident that the weather would derail Christopher and Ford's weekly golf meetup. "In lieu of golf this week, would you and your family like to come over for dinner tomorrow night?" Christopher texted Ford on Friday afternoon. "We're having a few friends over, and if the rain lets up in time, we'll grill some burgers."

"Great," he texted back. "I'll bring my wife."

The Fords arrived at Christopher's house on Saturday night. Wonderful smells wafted through the house.

"It smells amazing in here!" said Ford. "This is my wife, Rebecca."

"Nice to meet you! Come on out back and meet my wife, Michelle."

The rain cleared and turned to a light overcast, which meant a beautiful evening for a barbecue. A small group of people gathered on the deck. Everyone mingled, played some backyard games, and had an all-around good time before it was time to eat.

"Fancy meeting you here. How've you been?" said Terrence, shaking Ford's hand warmly.

"Ford, you remember Terrence from the course," said Christopher.

"Of course," said Ford. "Good to see you again."

"Christopher's been updating me about your golf games-slash-consultations. Sounds like you're having way too much fun talking about work. Christopher loves to talk about work."

"Fun is non-negotiable," joked Ford. "It's the most important for sure."

The men chatted for a while about a few things, catching up. Eventually, the conversation steered toward Christopher's company. "So, you're the VP of training and recruiting at the company, correct?" Ford asked Terrence.

"I am," he replied. "For five years now. What started as a part-time responsibility coordinating tech training for three people has morphed into a full-time gig, ensuring our people get educated on the latest and greatest."

"Let me ask you, are you more a CFO or CEO when it comes to training employees?" asked Terrence.

Ford responded, "I'm not sure I understand the question."

"Oh, sorry," said Terrence. Then he continued, "Have you heard the story of the CEO and CFO who were having the conversation about training. The CFO says, 'What happens if we train our people and they leave? We end up wasting all that money.' The CEO then says, 'What happens if we don't train them and they stay?'" He added, "I find that most executives fall into either a CFO or CEO camp on investing in training."

Ford chuckled then said, "That's a good one. I definitely fall into the CEO camp. I'm a big believer in just-in-time training as the research shows that the sooner people apply the information learned, the more they retain it. I know you might find this hard to believe, but I have three items I recommend all companies nail around training."

Terrence grinned, then he said, "Let's hear them."

Ford started, "Get the following three items nailed, and your value skyrockets with your people.

- Technical or skill-based education is a given (it is the cost of admission)
- Train on HOW the business works
- Create a learning culture

He continued, "I always stress that it's important that organizations train their people on how the business operates and what they can do to contribute and maximize value across the 3 Cs (Customers, Colleagues, and Company) for everyone, not just the technical requirements for doing their job. Technical competence is the price of admission, but business acumen provides a multiplying return on value."

"Sure," said Terrence.

"For example, if I'm running a manufacturing plant that produces brake pads for minivans, I would train my people on how to run the manufacturing equipment effectively, with the highest quality and in the safest manner. But I'd also want to make sure they understand the core business we're in."

Terrance smiled at Christopher then looked back at Ford.

"What happens if one brake pad out of 1,000,000 fails? That is 1/1,000th of a percent point failure, but it's also one real human life that could be put at risk.

As a brake manufacturer, we supply safety, not just brake pads. So, if everyone knows this, they put more energy and care into safety. All of the team members would know that we design, engineer, manufacture, and sell safety."

The listeners nodded along to the story.

"If one of those things fails, it can have an impact not only on human life but on the company's bottom line, and also on everyone's personal wealth or well-being. Don't forget our colleagues and friends we work with. The more you train this way, the more the team knows how their particular job affects the overall company, the overall customer, and their colleagues."

"Sure," said Christopher. "But is this the same mindset for non-life-and-death scenarios?"

"Absolutely. Another example is with a professional services company I worked with. Most of their projects were hourly, and the consultants were very aware that they needed to keep the project running on time, on budget, and on scope, because that provided the maximum value to the customer."

Christopher listened intently.

"Of course, their customers needed their projects on time and on budget, but sometimes a project would have a technical issue that required it to veer off track or created added hours to complete. Instead of keeping it within the scope of their own training and department, they needed to escalate that information. They found two things:

- People didn't want to escalate problems because they didn't want to contribute to an increase in the budget.
- When they buried issues until the last minute or until after a project went live, once those problems became known, it always ended up costing more to the customer (not to mention the costs to my client's reputation by not escalating until it was too late).

Ford continued, "No one wants to hear bad news, but it's always better to hear it up-front. You'd rather know that you need a $300 brake job on your car during a monthly inspection than learning your brakes were bad after you're unable to stop while you're driving."

"Well, when you put it that way…" Terrence laughed.

"Right?" said Ford with a grin. "But it's understandable why people are reluctant to be the guy who has to raise the issue. It's important to understand why it's a good idea to be that guy sometimes," he said. "In another instance, a consulting company didn't want to bother their consultants with knowing how to sell because that was the sales peoples' job."

"Isn't that kinda true, though?" asked Christopher.

"Well, of course it's the salespeople's job to sell. But they found that when the consulting engineers were taught what to be aware of when it came to either the types of things clients needed to buy or what type of devices they needed—in other words, things salespeople should be responsible for—their advice carried more weight than if it came from a salesperson."

"That makes sense," said Terrance.

"So, let's say a salesperson is trying to sell you something, like a $4,000 server. You may assume that it's just the salesperson trying to sell you something you may or may not need. Now, suppose the engineers or engineering team explains how a $4,000 server will help boost your performance, give you a better response time, and enhance your work. You're a lot more likely to get it approved for procurement in a quarter or even a tenth of the time than it might take if the sales team was selling it."

"That's incentive enough to cross-train your people," said Christopher.

"We found that by educating our front-line consultants, we increased our repeat business within our client base by eight times," said Ford. "The salespeople also had better, more realistic language to use to help sell the products to customers."

"Wow," said Terrence. "Ongoing education is so simple too."

"Another thing we looked at when approaching training was to create a culture of learning. I worked with another company where we set out to craft a space where colleagues were encouraged and wanted to learn, senior colleagues wanted to teach, and peers wanted to impart knowledge to each other as well."

Michelle handed Christopher a fresh drink.

"We made this is a self-motivating process. The colleagues wanted to learn for their own personal enhancement and do a better job for the end customers. They wanted to produce a better product or event for the end client, and also maybe look for a promotion by doing a better job."

"What's the process by which you make that work?" asked Terrence.

"Well, with this particular company, we created a whole in-house learning institute. We taught everything from how the business works to expected colleague behaviors for in the office and at client sites. Senior individuals taught those classes, and additional education was available on the condition that the colleagues were in good standing to receive the education. It worked out so that people did a good job to get access to the education."

Terrance stepped in closer to the speaker.

"Once they became senior members, they were encouraged, and they wanted to be selected to be an instructor within the in-house institute. It was a prestigious thing, and they received perks for doing that training as well."

Michelle brought the other guests another round of drinks and found a spot to listen to Ford's conversation.

Ford continued, "The entire process became a kind of a self-fulfilling prophecy where people wanted to learn, they were able to develop their own training content and materials, and they wanted to do the teaching when they became senior team members. The company found that, monetarily, it didn't require as much of an investment as they thought it would."

The listeners exchanged empty glasses for fresh drinks.

"People were willing to train and educate their co-workers for not much more money or even for no additional money in some cases. People would use and attend orientation and classes on their own time because they saw the value both personally and professionally. It created a unique culture of learning."

Michelle handed Ford a fresh glass as well.

"When I'm reviewing a company's approach to training, I also look at their approach to their internal operational tools. A quick backstory about why I look at training and tools at the same time is that I was with a company once that spent a ton of money training people on a new sales CRM. In addition to training the people on the new CRM, they spent money on purchasing the system and implementing the solution. As I dug more into the details, I found out that this was the third 'new' CRM system in five years. They always were convinced that a new technology tool or the latest system would solve their problems. So, my advice regarding spending money on the latest technology tool is to get the following correct first:

- Have your best practice defined first, then automate or improve.
- Have a single source of truth.
- Have an easy button for entering and retrieving data.

He continued, "It may not be necessary for companies to be on the leading edge of technology. They might not have to spend a fortune as long as the tools are efficient and effective for the colleagues to use. I've seen some companies with multiple tools that capture similar things or require their people to enter similar information into three different areas. You can see this pretty commonly in sales, but in project management too."

Terrence nodded along to the story and sipped his fresh drink.

"I've seen companies that required salespeople to enter call logs, data, and emails into a CRM system. In addition to that, they'll have a separate forecasting tool, like Excel or another kind of system. Then, once a quarter, they'll have to do a QBR (Quarterly Business Review) or presentation to management."

"Right," said Terrance.

"We coached them on implementing a more effective process with one integrated system that everyone uses. It didn't have to be the best Customer Relations Management (CRM), but it did need to allow for client communication capture across the enterprise—from sales, support, development, and so on."

Michelle checked her watch. "Food is almost ready," she whispered to Christopher.

Ford said, "This system should capture pipeline and forecasting information, and be something management would use. That way, rather than requiring a salesperson or account executive to create a separate deck, it just pulled information from the CRM. It was important to have the CRM optimized so the managers knew how to use it, they had solid dashboards, and it was easy to use information. Having everyone use the same tools for the same purpose reduces redundancy," he said as he looked to Christopher.

"Fascinating," said Christopher, who then called his guests to the table. Dinner and non-business conversation lasted well into the evening, and cleanup developed into a team effort.

"See? Much more efficient when everyone chips in, right?" said Ford.

"Listen to him, Christopher!" joked Michelle.

It got late, and the guests exchanged numbers as they got ready to leave. "I enjoyed the conversation, and you gave me a lot of ideas to look into on Monday when I get back to the office," Terrance said to Ford.

"I'm looking forward to seeing if and how we can apply these ideas to our current environment," replied Christopher with a laugh.

Terrence said his goodbyes, and Ford was on his way out the door when Christopher stopped him.

"I wanted to thank you for all the great advice. It's been helpful," he said.

"As long as you keep footing my golf habit, I'm perfectly happy to talk about it," said Ford with a smile.

"You got it. See you next Saturday," said Christopher.

6 | *Tools & Training*

The next morning, Christopher pulled out his notebook and recorded his notes on Tools & Training based on his conversation with Ford.

TOOLS & TRAINING NOTES

1. Train all colleagues on how the business works.
   - All colleagues understand how the company's finances work (how it makes money, what affects profit, what money is spent on, etc.)
   - All colleagues understand how to make better decision balancing three 3 Cs (company, customers, colleagues)
   - All colleagues understand how all departments fit together and affect each other

2. Create a culture of learning.
   - Develop a learning center of excellence
   - Inspire colleagues to teach others
   - Create a reward system

3. Focus on efficient tools.
   - There should be one source of truth
   - Get the efficient process right before choosing a tool
   - There's no need to spend dollars on the latest "hot" products

CHAPTER 7

ALIGNMENT OF THE ORGANIZATION

- If everyone is moving forward together, then success takes care of itself.
  - Henry Ford

- Action expresses priorities.
  - Mahatma Gandhi

- Build for your team a feeling of oneness, of dependence on one another and of strength to be derived by unity.
  - Vince Lombardi

The week following the barbecue was hectic for Christopher. He had been in meetings all week and forgot to ask his assistant to book a tee time for Saturday. He texted Ford Friday morning to let him know there were no available slots for their usual game.

7 | Alignment of the Organization

"Bummer," he responded. "Hey—you work downtown, right?"

Ford suggested the duo meet downtown at a local pub after work. By the time six o'clock rolled around, Christopher was ready to go. He walked the three blocks to a spot called Cass Street, the go-to spot for after-work beers. Ford was sitting at a high-top by the bar.

They talked about the football game on the TV above the bar, and Ford thanked Christopher for having them over the weekend before.

"My wife had a wonderful time," replied Christopher. "We'll have to do it more often."

After the usual pleasantries, Ford asked about Christopher's recent workweek. "How is it going with the plans you laid out in your off-sight strategic planning sessions?" asked Ford.

"Recently, we had a little bit of a disconnect between sales and delivery," replied Christopher. "Some of the reports indicated that a few customers didn't receive what they expected when they expected it. There are some issues of misalignment between departments."

"Anything else?" asked Ford.

"Well," said Christopher, "there is another issue, which was a smaller, lingering issue that is now becoming more pressing. It looks like Karen—our West Coast sales VP—is either an incompetent leader or is working against us on two of our corporate rocks for the quarter."

"I'm sure you know this, but those are monster issues, with either option being a major fatal flaw," said Ford.

"I do. Any suggestions?" Christopher asked.

Ford took a long drink from the local craft IPA, then said, "Let's circle back to Karen a bit later. You do need to address that bad apple, but instead, let's start with the blueprint to getting the whole organization aligned."

"Agreed," said Christopher.

"There's certainly a blueprint," replied Ford, who then listed his three key points:

1. Create a healthy executive team.
2. Align the 3 Cs (customer, colleague, and company).
3. Drive the entire organization toward the big rocks.

"It all starts with the healthy executive team. If your executive team is not aligned and healthy, you'll never have success in the long term," he added. "A healthy team is one that has trust, accountability, open and direct communications, and embraces good conflict."

Christopher bent his elbow for another frosty sip.

"An aligned team is a team that understands that the group goal is more important than individual goals, that team members support each other and understand

7 | Alignment of the Organization

how their strengths and weakness benefit the team, and an aligned team is energetically focused on what is important." He added, "For example, if you're on a rowing team and people are rowing in different directions, the boat will either spin and go nowhere, or zig-zag around and still go everywhere but the finish line. Obviously, that's not what anyone wants."

"No way to win a race," joked Christopher.

"Definitely not. Or, as another example, take a Formula-1 racing team. For the team to be healthy, everyone needs to drive toward one goal: win the race. If the mechanics build a car that can move the fastest, but the car still doesn't win races, the mechanical team fails with everyone else."

Christopher nodded along.

"If the driver can't out-drive the other drivers, then they fail along with the rest of the team. If the scouting and strategy teams don't put together the right drivers or create the right strategy to set them up to win, no one wins. No matter how well the strategists determine when to pit, when to rotate out or change tires, or how to direct the drivers, no one wins. No matter how great the driver is, no matter how skilled the mechanics, and so on. So, unless everyone is working together and is firmly aligned, the unit fails together," said Ford.

"Can you elaborate a little on what you're talking about when you say a healthy team?" asked Christopher.

"Well, a healthy team doesn't have politics. They're not at odds with each other, and they don't exist in silos, for a start," said Ford. "Take, for example, the Detroit Tigers of 2014. Talented players packed the team. Of the nine they had on the field, six (66 percent) were all-stars, including Miguel Cabrera, a two-time MVP and triple crown winner. The pitching staff included five all-star pitchers and four were Cy Young awarded pitchers."

Christopher looked skeptical.

Ford noticed the look. "Sounds like the perfect team, right? Well, that team lost in a sweep in the American League Championship Series. The 2012 and 2013 teams of mostly the same all-star players lost the World Series and the ALCS. While fans and sportswriters will debate the reasons they lost, the moral of the story is you need to be aligned and healthy. All-star individuals don't win championships."

Christopher sipped his drink.

"Some teams may have only one all-star player, or even just one strong player, but if the whole team clicks and gets together to execute a common goal, which is to win, that will be the team more likely to win championships."

"I see," said Christopher.

"Another interesting fact is that within four years, 90 percent of the players and a pitcher went on to win World Series championships with other teams. You need not only the right players—or colleagues—but also the right team to be great."

"Any suggestions on how to improve team alignment for our team?" asked Christopher.

"First, you need to ensure the team is healthy. Then you can ensure they are aligned. Both activities are journeys and not a switch that can be flipped, so be prepared to live the process. Also, every time the team is changed—new hires, departures, terminations—the dynamic will change, and you may need to undertake some of these steps again. You will find some individuals are more receptive to healthy teams than others, and everyone will follow your lead."

"So, in addition to being aligned to work toward one goal, everyone involved needs to get along, in essence?" asked Christopher.

"It's more than that," said Ford. "Getting along is important to everyone. No one wants to work with people they dislike, but behaviors like trust without fear of conflict, commitment, and accountability need to be mirrored from the top down. Behave the way you'd like to see people behave throughout your organization."

"Right," said Christopher. "I've certainly seen better teams come from better coaching and leadership accountability."

"To build trust, I suggest incorporating the following exercises into your monthly meeting:

- The Personal Sharing exercise
- The Start/Stop exercise

- The Johari's Window exercise
- Any one of many Personality Profiling assessments, such as DiSC or PI

The key to these exercises is to make them a process and create a rhythm to the discussions. Avoid the trap of making these onetime activities."

Christopher jotted down the recommendations.

"Next, I would suggest incorporating activities that promote good conflict, such as mining for good conflict in meetings, asking for real-time permission, and defining rules of engagement for business discussions. After this, I would incorporate cascading messages and agreed on commitments to the end of all staff meetings. The last step is to put accountability techniques into your daily habits. These include behavioral and public accountability methods."

Christopher made a few more notes on these various suggestions.

Ford noticed Christopher's expression. "I can email you some additional books and articles[1] on the topic of team alignment."

"Great. Is there anything in particular you told people to focus on when getting their teams on the right path to alignment? I mean, other than the quarterly rocks and their KPIs?" asked Christopher.

---

[1] Visit www.aspensummitgroup.com/details to download a sample document.

7 | Alignment of the Organization

"Once aligned and focused on the company's rocks and KPIs, it is vital that people make sound strategic decisions. The best advice I was ever given regarding sound decision making was provided early in my career, and it was to balance the three Cs:

1. Customer
2. Colleague
3. Company

Ford added, "Every decision that's made within the company, regardless of the type of decision it is—strategy, customer engagement, colleague engagement, delivery and execution of R&D, product development, product deployment—ought to be aligned around all three Cs. When that's in place, you've got a healthy organization ready to execute at maximum capacity."

"It's about balance," said Christopher.

"Right," said Ford. "You want your customers to be happy, but you also want your team to be happy. And, of course, you want the company to be successful."

"I see," said Christopher.

"Some classic examples of this balance is colleague compensation. All team members would love to have a million-dollar salary, but to do this, you would need to charge your customers exorbitant prices. This would not be sustainable, and the company would go out of business."

"Everyone loses," said Christopher.

"Exactly. So, wages that allow colleagues to be fairly compensated and promotes good retention of the best allows for customers to pay a fair price and receive the benefits of the product or service and allows the company to make a profit to generate long-term success."

"That makes sense."

"Now, some days, weeks, or months feel temporarily out of balance, but if all the stakeholders—customers, colleagues, company—know that balance will occur over time, you get better decisions and a clearer path to success."

"Of course."

"You can find examples of this in plenty of areas, whether it's delivery or customer service. But, if you overpromise your customer, they expect a certain level of service or quantity of product. If you under-deliver, of course, they won't be happy. If they're not happy, they don't buy, and your company suffers."

Christopher looked back to Ford.

"Employees suffer because they have less opportunity for advancement, or—again, worst-case scenario—your company goes out of business, and no one has a job anymore at all. When the three Cs align over the long haul, you have a good, equitable, balanced organization paving the way for teams to operate at maximum efficiency."

7 | Alignment of the Organization

"That's definitely something we need at HealthCloud," the listener responded.

"I like to visualize it like a rubber band stretched out between your fingers into a triangle. This triangle has three equal sides and equal angles, but the rubber band has flexibility, so if you have to move or adjust, sometimes your triangle won't stay a perfect isosceles. It may have some weird angles or look bent in parts, but the three points always stay anchored without breaking the rubber band. The goal is to keep those points strong and try to keep your triangle balanced over the long haul."

Christopher finished his drink.

Ford finished off his beer and ordered another round. "Once the executive team is aligned and the company is balancing the three Cs, the glue that makes alignment stick is driving the organization toward achieving the big rocks."

"These are the same rocks we established in the strategic plan, right?"

"Yes," said Ford. "You want to make sure that all your actions, behaviors, reporting, and communications are driving the whole organization toward those rocks. Achieving the rocks will drive the organization toward reaching its goals. The key to driving the organization toward the rocks is communication. Communication needs to be clear, direct, transparent, timely, and consistent. Most importantly, this messaging must be delivered through multiple channels and with the rhythm of a never-ending drumbeat."

The bartender presented two new drinks.

"Christopher, you might be too young to remember the movie the *Ten Commandments* with Charlton Heston," said Ford.

"I know the one. They show it on TV every year," Christopher said.

"Yep." Ford continued, "Well, there is a scene where Charles Heston is rowing in the bowels of the boat. At the front of the ship is the taskmaster beating the drum to the rhythm everyone is expected to row. The reason I use this example is your messaging about what is important about the rocks needs to be as consistent, reliable, and as predictable as the rhythm of the drumbeat."

"Interesting," said Christopher.

"Communication centering around team member awareness of what the rocks are for that quarter, and how to drive toward that with balance, is key. This communication, must not be a one-time occurrence."

Christopher rotated in his seat.

Ford began, "The constant reinforcement of communication through metrics and KPIs should happen daily and weekly. This communication should come from and be reinforced by management through discussions with their colleagues about their focus and effort throughout the quarter."

7 | *Alignment of the Organization*

"That makes so much sense," said Christopher. As the duo sipped on their final beer for the evening, Christopher's watch vibrated with a message from his wife. "Looks like I need to be heading home. Still need to pick up steaks for dinner."

"Lucky you," said Ford. "Let's try for a round next week?"

"Golf or beer?" joked Christopher.

"Both!" exclaimed Ford.

That evening, Christopher pulled out his notebook and recorded his notes on Alignment based on his conversation with Ford.

ALIGNMENT NOTES

1. A healthy and aligned executive team is necessary. Failure to do so is death.
   - Team acts as one team and is rowing in the same direction
   - Focus on health (no silos, no politics, no personal agendas)
   - Build strong teams per 5 dysfunctions

2. Align the 3 Cs: Customer, Colleagues, and Company.
   - Balanced them over time
   - Apply a flexible approach
   - Never waiver and explain decisions publicly

3. Full organization driving to the big Rocks.
   - Communicated via multiple channels and on a predictable business rhythm
   - Share information with transparency
   - Use a clear, direct communication style

CHAPTER 8

INTEGRATE THE PEOPLE SYSTEMS

- If you think hiring professionals is expensive, try hiring amateurs.
  ### - Anonymous

- Human Resources isn't a thing we do. It's the thing that runs our business.
  ### - Steve Wynn, Wynn Las Vegas

- Regard your soldiers as your children, and they will follow you into the deepest valleys; look on them as your own beloved sons, and they will stand by you even unto death.
  ### - Sun Tzu

The duo met for their usual tee time the following week, but Christopher noticed a laser focus in Ford's golf game. Throughout the day, the young man drafted off Ford's enthusiastic match, and both players ended up near their personal best scores for the day.

"What a game," exclaimed Christopher after the final hole.

"I really felt something today," said Ford. "I think all of this practice has changed my view of these casual Saturdays."

After loading up clubs in both their vehicles, Ford offered to buy Christopher a round of beers at the clubhouse bar. Christopher jumped on the offer.

Ford handed Christopher a twenty-dollar bill. "I still can't get over it," he reiterated. "You were really on fire today. Congratulations on a new personal best score."

"I think it's the practice and a few lucky bounces," replied Christopher. "My whole game was working today. Somedays I drive the ball well, but chip or putt awful. Other days, I cannot hit a fairway but scramble and putt well. It's nice when it all works together."

"Of course, but I will be trying to win my twenty back next week," said Ford as he wiped the frosty foam from his mouth at the bar.

"I would expect nothing less. And good luck, you'll need it," said Christopher as both guys laughed. He continued, "While we look at the menu, let me hear about another piece of your methodology for operational success."

"Sure thing. As you know, I'm a work geek," Ford said. "Just like when all the aspects of your golf game work together to produce a great score, you need to ensure you are integrating all your human systems within the company. Most companies understand the benefits of integrating various computer and data systems. So, what I focus on is integrating the people side, how people act and behave while working."

"I see."

"Before I explain my three main areas for integration, I want to touch on *why* I am focusing on how people act, what they do, how they communicate, and all the other non-skills-based activities. We have all heard the term, 'It only takes one bad apple to spoil a bunch.' I think we all understand this and agree with it, but you would be surprised how often companies live with a bad apple or apples. In short, don't fall into one of these traps:

- Bob is our best support tech. He can figure out any issue, so we will 'manage around' his client communications issues.
- I'll replace Jim as soon as I find a qualified replacement.
- Our clients love Sue. We will 'work on' her negative attitude. Again.

Ford added, "Have you ever heard the phrase, 'No good deed goes unpunished?'"

"I have, along with firsthand experience of the damage it can do," said Christopher.

8 | Integrate the People Systems

"This is especially true when it comes to colleagues whose behaviors do not match your corporate standards," said Ford.

"But what about managing behavior in addition to performance? Sometimes the two don't line up. You can have a high performer with a lousy attitude. What do you do about that?"

Ford replied, "You integrate healthy behavior into hiring, reviews, and promotions. During those unfortunate times when you've done everything you can to help someone succeed, but there's no alternative, you counsel people out of the organization. This means ensuring that people are promoted and rewarded for positive, healthy behavior, and not promoted or rewarded for behavior that brings down the positive energy of their peers and the people around them."

"You need to hire, promote, and fire for the same metrics," confirmed Christopher.

"Correct." Ford continued, "The three areas of human integration I suggest targeting first are:

1. Aligned incentives
2. Actions that exceed customer exceptions
3. Personal energy plans for everyone

"Let's start with tackling the issue of creating incentive programs that are aligned and behavior-based. The incentive programs for individual team members must be consistent with the incentive programs for any group. They also need to be aligned with the company's rocks, initiatives, yearly goals, and—last, but not least—with the incentive programs of management."

The waitress refilled their drinks. Christopher and Ford smiled with approval.

"I've worked with a couple of companies where management's incentive programs were not aligned with incentive programs for the colleagues, and incentive programs for different departments were different. This usually ends up with departments at odds and management and colleagues at odds with each other," continued Ford.

"Right," said Christopher. "That makes sense."

"I've found that, in general, most people will follow the money in their day-to-day activities. What their incentives and rewards are will reflect how they behave and act daily. At one company, the sales department hit their quota and incentives, but the company missed its profit goal."

Christopher nodded along.

"The problem with this company was that the type of deals and the profit of the deals did not support an overall healthy company profit. The following year when incentives were aligned, everyone pulled in the same direction."

The waiter checked in on the duo and moved to the next group.

"Take the following classic oversimplified example: Sales bonuses are based on top-line revenue. Delivery bonuses are based on customer satisfaction, and the executive team's bonuses are based on company profit. This produces the following results:

- Sales discounts and over-promises in the contract to win more easy sales
- Delivery is forced to work overtime to deliver on the contract, and they also provide free out of scope work to 'make the customer happy'
- The executive team cuts the education and system upgrades to make corporate earnings because of low-profit sales and 'free work' done to delight the customer

"But when all teams have aligned incentives, the following happens: Sales wins deals without discounts and writes correctly scoped contracts. Delivery can deliver the product without overtime and provide outstanding services, which results in increased repeat business. The executive team can fund inertial initiatives and pay all incentives because teams are aligned."

Christopher sipped his drink.

"This might be an oversimplified example, but we have all seen examples of this type of aligned incentives. Stay diligent to aligning compensation, and don't be afraid of rocking the boat or touching a golden goose."

The listener thought about his teams back at the office.

"The second part of aligned incentives is including behavior criteria in the colleague review process. In most companies, this yearly process is what drives salary increases and promotions. This process must include behavior-based criteria."

"Ok, I think I see where you are going with this," said Christopher.

"At many companies, the typical team member review is some sort of three page, fill in the blank, essay-style of review. It is not metrics-driven, so the colleague has no real, tangible number to reach for. Therefore, the expectations of management regarding performance isn't as clear as it could be."

"I see."

"Managers hate these reviews because they always take a ton of effort. Colleagues don't like them because the feedback is never timely, and the goals are somewhat ambiguous."

"How did you improve it?"

"We sampled everything. We changed the annual reviews from three pages of essay-style questions and answers to five questions that were quantitative in areas that both the colleagues and the manager could elaborate upon and give examples for. They also weren't just narrative."

Christopher glanced down at the menu.

"We established three behavior-based measurements and two technical or skills-based metrics to develop a score-based system for their reviews. Once we rolled those out, colleagues were happier because it clarified what they needed to do to be successful and explained the expectations for advancement both within the company and with the customers. Managers liked them because they were faster and more targeted with respect to how they chose to promote and advance people within the company."

"Faster generally feels better for all colleagues."

"Faster and better service. Once you have your incentives aligned, you want to focus on promoting actions that exceed customer exceptions. Services is the great equalizer. Outstanding service can make average products surge in sales and can cause great products to sink. I have never heard someone say, 'I stopped using that product, but I loved the service.' Usually, you might hear the opposite when someone says, 'I'll pay a little more or drive out of my way for excellent service.'"

"That's certainly been the case for me," said Christopher as he ordered another round.

"When I was younger and received my first big bonus check, I wanted to buy a new car. I visited an upscale Germany-based car company. When I walked in, they saw a young kid not dressed in a suit. They made me wait, and my first impression of the dealer's staff was that they were a snobby, unfriendly, rude sales team making me feel unworthy of a test drive."

The waiter removed the empty pint glasses.

"The next car dealer I visited was a competing brand with a three-letter name. When I walked in, they immediately greeted me—both dealers were equally busy at the time—and offered me a test drive almost instantly. Well, I bought the car for cash at the second dealer and made a promise never to buy that first brand of car. To this day, I have never visited their dealerships again. I tell you this story to illustrate how important customer experience and service is. You may never get a second chance."

"That's a ton of money if you think about the lifetime of a customer."

"Absolutely," said Ford. "In general, it does not cost extra to provide good service. Most companies have corporate value statements with multiple desired corporate values. Most certainly, everyone must live and behave by these values. I suggest taking it to another level with defining what service levels are acceptable and then defining what is exceeding expectations."

"Basically, make sure everyone knows service is important," reiterated Christopher.

"It's true for everything," said Ford. "Think about it. 'We will make and cook you a pizza,' versus 'We will deliver that pizza for a fee, but save you time,' versus 'We will deliver that pizza for free,' versus 'We will deliver the pizza in 30 minutes or it's free,' versus 'The store manager will personally call you if your pizza is late and the next pizza is free.'"

"You're creating a story for the customer as well," said Christopher.

8 | Integrate the People Systems

"Once you define what is expected, the next step is to promote and incentivize people to what is going above and beyond. Going above and beyond will become the new standard. Also, don't stop with traditional customer-based service levels. Include every department and internal and external customer. Once defined, over-communicate those standards. Provide examples and training. Then promote and reward those team members that excel and eliminate those who do not."

"It's all a service industry," Christopher said to himself.

"The last and most important aspect of integrating the system is energy. I want to make sure every person is bringing high energy to their job and putting energy into the right activities. Now, this may sound counterintuitive, but follow along. I don't want to 'motivate' my team members, and it is not my job to 'motivate' the staff."

The listener, deep in thought, swirled his drink.

"What I want to do is provide meaningful work, tools, education, rewards, social systems, and so on, to provide the right overall work environment. When this exists, the colleagues motivate themselves. When someone else motivates me, it is short-term, but when I am self-motivated to do something, it sticks long term with a greater positive impact. I refer to this as creating the right work energy and providing the right systems to allow the teams to bring the energy all day long."

Christopher listened.

"At my past companies, we set out to create positive energy for all team members and get them to a point where they looked forward to coming to work. We needed positive energy when servicing our customers, positive energy when producing widgets, or positive energy when interviewing other colleagues to join. The more positivity that goes around, the more infectious it becomes, which leads to higher energy levels all around. The positivity must be genuine, sincere, and meaningful."

The waiter sat two more drinks in front of the duo.

"People deserve to enjoy and find meaning within their work. If they enjoy the work and the people they work with, they'll derive more satisfaction in the positive outcomes and results their customers see. The more satisfaction they derive, the more successful they become. The more successful they become, the more positive energy they bring to the building."

"Like a cycle," said Christopher as he sipped his drink.

"Exactly. These are the things that create happy colleagues, which in turn creates a positive corporate culture, which leads to a more productive corporate culture."

"That sounds awesome, but how do you develop energy for colleagues? What does that look like?" asked Christopher.

8 | Integrate the People Systems

"We began creating Personal Energy Plans for each person. The PEP provides each person with a roadmap for how to focus their energy for maximum success. The PEPs are like personal dashboards for what to do each day, week, month, quarter, and year. They contained personal KPIs for the three Cs (Customer, Colleagues, and Company)."

"Sure," he said.

"Everyone needs a daily, weekly, and monthly number they're striving for, whether it's a sales quota, a certain number of widgets produced, a customer satisfaction score, or a certain number of interviews completed. Whatever it might be, everyone needs to know they have a goal that supports the goal of their team, their company, and supports increased shareholder value."

The waiter stopped by the table. "How about two burgers?" asked Christopher.

Ford nodded in approval and continued, "When we talked to the colleagues, we also overwhelmingly found that they hated the year-long process of receiving reviews and feedback. Think about it. You get a year's worth of feedback all at once, so something you did eleven months ago that caused a problem or was wrong is just now being talked about. They're just now learning about it in their yearly performance review, and that's keeping them from getting a raise or a promotion."

"I wouldn't be too happy about that," said Christopher.

"No one was. So, when we developed a colleague PEP, in addition to setting an agreed-upon, realistic, goal-based number, we implemented reviews and feedback every three months or at the end of every project, whichever came first. This reduced the time elapsed in-between reviews and feedback substantially."

Christopher nodded.

"If people's behaviors and skill sets are enhanced constantly on a real-time basis, or as often as possible, you'll get a better output and happier colleagues," said Ford.

"Makes sense to me," said Christopher, sipping his drink. "It's the same as scouting reports or weekly data in any professional sports league."

"It's even the same thing with kids in school," Ford continued. "They learn and do homework. Their homework is graded. That's their daily goal. They know every day how they're doing based on the number associated with that daily homework. They may then have a weekly quiz to measure what they've learned and achieved during that week. Now they know how they're doing weekly based on that grade. Then maybe monthly exams or quarterly exams roll around."

"Right," said Christopher. "So, it's the same thing in a work environment."

Ford added, "It takes constant back-and-forth learning and feedback to achieve a good grade or hit a goal. Imagine if those students were tested only once a year but were given no homework, no quizzes, no tests, and no grades up until that final exam. They wouldn't know if they were successful until the very end of the year."

"Well, that's setting someone up for failure in a way. They're blind," said Christopher.

"Blind," reiterated Ford. "There would be no way to help them grow or modify their behavior to set them up for success. So, for the company, we moved the reviews to the end of each project or every three months, whichever came first. People loved it both on the managers' and team members' sides, and we made sure that there were three-month goals and one-year goals or objectives for the employee to develop. We made sure there was an educational component, a team component, and a personal component to the goals for each person."

Christopher nodded and took another swig of his drink.

"In summary, use Personal Energy Plans along with personal KPIs. Include timely and real-time performance feedback, along with behavior metrics."

The men finished their drinks as the waiter placed two meals in front of the duo. Christopher grabbed the silverware in front of him as Ford's words started to sink in.

"Let's dig in," said Ford.

The Focused CEO

After dinner, Christopher pulled out his notebook and recorded his notes on Integration based on his conversation with Ford.

**INTEGRATION OF
THE HUMAN SYSTEMS NOTES**

1. Ensure incentive programs are aligned.
   - Align programs for the individual, team, management, and department
   - Accept nothing less than exceeding the customers' expectations
   - Hiring, promotions, and terminations are based on behavior and skill-based criteria

2. Provide an outstanding customer experience.
   - Service matters. It is your trump card for success
   - Make a good 1st impression. You may never get a second chance
   - Exceed the customers' expectations ALWAYS

3. Personal energy plans (PEPs).
   - Every person has a daily number (KPI)
   - Reviews should be simple, specific, and skill/behavior-based
   - Reviews happen in real time or every three (3) months

CHAPTER 9

LEAD & LEVERAGE

- No man will make a great leader who wants to do it all himself or to get all the credit for doing it.
  - **- Andrew Carnegie**

- Earn your leadership every day.
  - **- Michael Jordan**

- The greatest leader is not necessarily the one who does the greatest things. He is the one that gets the people to do the greatest things.
  - **- Ronald Reagan**

Christopher awoke to the sound of pots and pans clanging in the kitchen and the aroma of bacon tempting him down the stairs. It took him a few minutes of fumbling to find his phone on the dresser. When he could focus his eyes enough to read his phone, he realized it was 9 a.m. He began to sit up when his wife appeared at the door.

"Happy birthday!" she exclaimed. "I didn't know if you'd be hungry, but there was no way I was going to wake you up."

Christopher climbed out of bed, threw on his workout clothes, and made his way down to the kitchen.

"Looks great, thanks!" said Christopher as he sat down at dove into his breakfast.

"It's nice when your birthday falls on a Saturday," she said. "What do you want to do for your birthday? Do you feel like doing anything in particular?"

After a quick workout, they settled on a domestic day of relaxation and working in the garden, then dinner at Christopher's favorite restaurant, which served fresh seafood. He reflected on the last 35 years of his life and how much of it he'd put into work. He loved his work, and he felt as if he was making a difference in the world through his achievements.

"Can't ask for much more than that," he told his wife as they marveled at the size of the tomatoes and cucumbers in the garden.

Later, they showered, got dressed, and phoned an Uber to get out for a night on the town. They decided to have cocktails before dinner at a nice piano bar they went to on their first date. During drinks, he noticed his wife checking her phone every few minutes.

He asked with a laugh, "Are you expecting a call?"

"No," she said. "Just don't want to be late for our reservation."

They finished their drinks and headed to the restaurant. It was a short walk from the bar, and the crowd outside made him glad his wife had made a reservation. They approached the hostess station. Christopher was puzzled when the hostess led them past the bustling tables to the back of the restaurant and down a long hallway.

The hostess opened the door to a room and gestured for them to enter. It was dark, but in a flash, the lights flipped on, and Christopher was bombarded by a loud "Surprise!" from his family and friends as they jumped out from behind the tables.

"Easy!" Christopher laughed. "I'm an old man. You're gonna give me a heart attack!" Christopher had never felt so loved, and he was even more pleasantly surprised to see Ford and his wife were amongst the group.

Eventually, the crowd thinned out until it was just Christopher, Michelle, Ford, and Rebecca. The server assured them they were welcome to stay as long as they liked. Since they had the room until closing time, they ordered coffee and after-dinner drinks to go with Christopher's leftover cake.

"How's work going?" Ford asked. "Or should this topic be off-limits for just this one evening out of the last 35 years?"

"Have at it, guys," said Michelle. "Rebecca and I have some catching up to do as well."

They talked about what had been happening recently at the company, and Christopher said he was confident about the direction they were headed. "We've been making some pretty impressive progress. Everyone's pulling together, and it looks like we'll be rolling out the new product on time, if not a little sooner. The shareholders are happy, so everyone's happy."

"Sounds like you've got some pretty sound leadership over there," said Ford. "That's a gift, for sure."

"I do," said Christopher. "I mean, no one is perfect, but everyone's committed, and we work well together."

Ford took a big bite of birthday cake. "I've worked at some companies with outstanding leadership. It's a gift to be a part of a team with a great leader, not only because it makes your job more enjoyable, but also because of all the things you're able to learn on the job."

Christopher looked at his friend for a minute, imagining all of the people he had worked with over the years. "What do you think makes a great leader?"

"Oh, everything that goes into being a great leader could take hours. Given that I only have one or two more drinks left in me, let me give you my top three attributes." Ford began, "First lead by example. Remove roadblocks and friction for your people and customers, and find your leadership sweet spot."

Christopher thought about the quick response.

"First and foremost, you have to get out of your office. Make sure your people *see* you out too. That way they know you're not locked in your office managing via email."

The listener sipped his wine.

"Engage with everyone where *they* work, socialize, and interact. If you're always calling people into your office to have meetings and conversations, try engaging and having meetings in the lunchroom, other offices, work areas, on the factory floor, or anywhere that makes you more accessible. People see you engaging where *they* perform, not just in your office."

"Makes sense."

"Include virtual walking around in this work from anywhere world. Call or Zoom with team members to talk about how you can help them. Avoid the temptation to always talk about 'the job.' Join or host virtual Zoom calls, lunch and learns, or virtual town halls, and engage in smart social media."

Christopher reached for another piece of cake.

"I think the extension of that is to lead by example," he continued. "Showing and demonstrating that everything you ask your people to do, you have done or currently do yourself. If you're asking the team to 'do whatever it takes' to get a project done, it is important they know you have done what it takes in the past and that you will be by their side the whole time."

"I've tried to do that as best I can, for sure," said Christopher.

"If it requires an all-nighter or some weekend work to get a job done, they'll know you've successfully done this many times in your life. They'll also know that you're right there with them through the process."

"I see."

"I worked for a tech company early in my career where we were rushing to get some code out to a client base. There was a whole team of fifteen people working on this project, and we had to pull an epic all-nighter to get it out on time. It wasn't only me, my co-workers, and our boss, but our boss's boss and his boss's boss were there to participate in the process throughout the night until we got it done."

Christopher turned to face Ford.

"Another time, we were getting out our largest bid proposal to a client. We were writing, drafting, re-writing, editing, and making sure this thing was the best that it could be right up to the deadline, and again, there were about eight of us that were working late into the night. Not only were the editors there, the tech team, the finance team, but the CEO of the company was right there with us too."

"This same principle applies anywhere, right?"

"Right. It could be in a manufacturing area where you ask someone to redo something they've already worked hard on. If they know that you showed that same dedication before you became a manager or executive, it means a lot. There's a saying I heard early on in my career: People follow people, not companies."

"I like that," said Christopher.

"If you have high employee satisfaction and engagement, it's most likely because the employees are engaged with each other and experiencing that together. Not because of some mystical culture that people can't see. It's the culture of the people and how they interact. People follow, or relate, to other people."

"I've had similar experiences," said Christopher. "I've seen managers who led by example and others who didn't. It feels vastly different to work for one over the other."

The laughter of their wives at the next table diverted their attention.

Ford smiled and swirled his wine in its glass, thoughtfully watching the legs around the inside drop to the bottom. "I think another big piece of leadership is eliminating friction and roadblocks," he said.

"What do you mean specifically when you say friction?" asked Christopher.

"Things like friction in the process," he clarified. "Problems that inhibit colleagues from contributing faster, being more productive, and bringing more energy to their jobs. It's not about creating bureaucracy. Rather, it's about eliminating those roadblocks and reducing the friction to get things done better and faster."

Christopher signaled for another round.

"One thing I like to do with teams is a start/stop exercise at different times of the year. I'd ask different people at different levels to tell me all things they think we should start doing or do more of and all things we should stop doing. I believe that the people doing the job every day know where the unnecessary bureaucracy is and where they can be more efficient. If you stop and listen, the things you should begin doing to be more effective will become apparent, as will the things you should stop doing to be more efficient."

The server dropped off two more drinks.

"If you are given multiple suggestions from multiple people doing the same job, you need to pay attention. Stop doing things immediately that make no sense to them, and begin immediately doing the things that they feel will improve the company."

"We've always put a priority on open communications between management and their teams. I've worked in environments where the management didn't seem to value the feedback of their people," said Christopher.

"Everyone probably has at some point in time. It's unavoidable, I think," said Ford. "Leveraging your leadership is so important. Leveraging can work at any organization level, but it's especially important for the founder of a company, CEO, or the executive team. I strongly suggest all executives create and utilized what I call a D.E.P., or Deep, chart."

"What is it?" asked Christopher.

"D.E.P. stands for Delegate, Educate, and Perform. The first thing is to create a three-column chart. Label the first column, 'activities,' label the second column 'expertise,' and label the third column 'love/hate.'"

Activities	Expertise	Love or hate

Ford continued, "Now, have each executive list in column one everything they do each day, week, month, and quarter. When the executive finished that list, fill in columns two and three. For column two, have them rate themselves 0-10 on their levels of expertise. With ten being a total expert and zero being no skills in the activity."

Christopher pictured the chart in his mind.

"For column three, have them rate themselves 0-10 on their levels of love or hate of that activity. With ten being they love performing the activity and zero being they hate performing the activity. When the chart is finished, we want to plot the activities on a 4-quadrant grid. The y-axis is the love/hate, and the x-axis is the expertise."

Delegate	Perform
Delegate	Educate others

"Got it," said Christopher.

"The executive should delegate everything on the left side of the grid. Everything on the bottom right, the executive should educate someone else to perform. The top right shows activities that the executive is an expert at and loves doing. This is where the executive should spend 80 percent of their time."

Christopher responded, "I've heard delegation described as 'Who, Not How,' meaning who can do this job for you, rather than spending your time learning something you don't really need to know."

"Exactly. I like that. I love being face-to-face with the customer, talking about their business and what they need to accomplish and then working with them on how our products and services can help them achieve their goals or solve a specific problem or challenge."

"I could've guessed that about you," said Christopher. "You're a pretty social guy."

"True, but you know what I hated doing? Logistics and supply chain. This is an example of something I would delegate to others on the management team. For something like data analysis, I would mentor or teach others on the team to perform. I'm good at it, but I don't enjoy doing it. So, I leverage myself to get maximum results with my time."

"I spend an odd amount of time planning company meals," joked Christopher.

"Again, focus 80-90 percent of your time in that top right quadrant."

"I'm going to do that for the task list I've got at home," Christopher laughed.

Ford laughed, "I don't think it'll work in that scenario." The friends finished their drinks, packed up the rest of the cake, and waited in front of the restaurant for their rides home.

"Thanks for such a great night!" Ford said to Michelle.

"Good birthday?" she asked as they stood on the side.

"Good birthday," Christopher confirmed with a smile.

9 | Lead & Leverage

The following day, Christopher pulled out his notebook and recorded his notes on Lead & Leverage based on his conversation with Ford.

LEAD & LEVERAGE NOTES

1. Leaders lead by example.
   - Manage by walking around
   - Engage on a personal level
   - Only ask people to do what you have done or will do

2. Leaders remove roadblocks, eliminate problems, and reduce friction.
   - Use the start/stop exercises (feedback as to what can be added or eliminated)
   - Help colleagues provide outstanding service to others
   - Help employees contribute faster

3. Leaders use the D.E.P. Chart.
   - Delegate what is not in your wheelhouse
   - Educate others on what you are an expert at
   - Perform those things you love and are great at

CHAPTER 10

THE RHYTHM OF BUSINESS

- Practice does not make perfect. Only perfect practice makes perfect.
  - Vince Lombardi

- The harder you work, the luckier you get.
  - Gary Player

- The eight laws of learning are explanation, demonstration, imitation, repetition, repetition, repetition, repetition, repetition.
  - John Wooden

Saturday rolled around, and Christopher was looking forward to playing golf. When he got to the course, he met up with Ford on the range. "From the look of those last few shots you hit, it looks like I might be in trouble today."

"Feeling good now—want to double our standard wager?" Ford asked.

"Sure thing. I have seen you putt. I think my money is safe," joked Christopher as they both laughed.

They finished hitting some balls and set out to play their round. "I enjoyed our chat last week at your birthday party," said Ford. "I'm glad things are better at work."

"No small thanks to you," said Christopher. "Your advice has been invaluable. Thank you."

"I enjoy helping. Just remember: it's a process of continuous improvement."

"I understand that it's a process, and I already see places my team is performing well at and places we can make improvements," said Christopher. "Are there more steps in the method?"

"There is one final key item," said Ford. "Do you remember when I mentioned the rhythm of business is an important part of making it all work?"

"I do," said Christopher. "Please tell me I don't have to sing?"

"All the concepts we've talked about need to be performed with a predictable business cadence and element of rhythm to tie it all together," said Ford. "It's important everyone understands why doing this will produce and drive home maximum results. With the correct rhythm, the concepts create a multiplier and catalyst effect within your organization."

"Right."

"We want to make sure we're practicing data-driven processes regularly; we have the right financial plan within our company; we have training optimized; we're aligned; we're integrating our human systems; we're leading and leveraging our teams; and we're all driving toward that strategy of where we want to go as an organization."

Christopher hit a bullet down the fairway.

"Rhythm is how we do these things every day, every month, every quarter, and every year. Doing something with rhythm is easier than doing something without a predictable schedule. I think taking care of yourself is a good example. I know from personal experience when I get into a rhythm of working out and eating healthy, it becomes easier. It makes me want to get up in the morning and exercise and eat right. If I skip a day or a week, that next day is a little harder. If I go on vacation and staying a week, starting back up after vacation is even harder. Staying on the analogy of working out, when you have a set rhythm to your exercise routine, it is much easier than when the workouts are random."

"I know exactly what you are saying," said Christopher. "I hit the gym every morning before work."

"And what happens if you skip a day?"

"It feels bad, and I crave getting back the next day."

"Right. The rhythm is what focuses you on the process of doing the right things every day. You have to practice the adage of getting right back on track if you get out of rhythm."

Christopher nodded. "I know what you mean. Habits aren't so easy to establish sometimes, but they're even harder to pick back up if you get off track."

"Exactly," said Ford. "I think an example that illustrates why rhythm is so important is the behavior of an average college student. Think about when you were back in college. If you crammed for a test, chances are you didn't retain the knowledge long term. So, cramming for a test is like drawing a slow arc, or a hockey stick that's somewhat flat at the beginning but shoots up at the end."

"That's the truth," he said.

"That's what happens when you cram. You don't retain the information you study. Twenty-four or forty-eight hours before the test, you try to do all the memorizing and studying within that brief period of time. You may achieve the result of having some of the knowledge in time for the test, but the retention and ability to use it or repeat it long term is usually not there."

Christopher hit another perfect drive down the fairway.

"You're on fire," said Ford. "On the other hand, people who do homework, who study, who read the assignments and do a little every day have a gradual arc of learning. It becomes a habit and a rhythm to study and learn the material. Those students usually do so much better on their exams and retain the knowledge longer than those who cram. While I learned that lesson, I don't necessarily know that I practiced it as well as I should have, being a typical college student. I'd phase in and out of good habits, depending on which semester I was in at school. What really made this stick—doing things with rhythm—was in my first job."

Christopher and Ford hopped in the cart.

"At my first job out of college, I was a coder at a software company. We wrote medical billing and records software for the medical industry. Doing my coding, I had to write computer programs and document my code. A lot of programmers would code for a month and say, 'I'm gonna go back and do my documentation at the end.'"

"Sure."

"Whenever I did that, I ran into problems. I had to cram to get it done, which resulted in sub-par quality documentation, and my bosses could tell. Even if it was adequate for my boss, I started to realize that it was easier if I wrote my documentation daily. If I had to go back to a piece of code I wrote six months or a year later, those sections I documented well, I could understand, fix, and debug much quicker than I could have if I'd written crappy documentation or none at all."

"Daily, incremental work," said Christopher.

"I learned to do my documentation every day as I went. I wrote the code, then wrote what I was doing. In some cases, I would write the documentation first, then write the code. I found that my documentation quality went up, as did my compliance with documenting all aspects of what I was doing. Of course, this seemed like a lifetime ago, but it's a lesson that stuck with me well beyond and has served me well," said Ford.

"Makes sense," said Christopher.

"Another example where you can see the secret sauce of rhythm is when you compare the business world to the athletic world. Have you heard the term 'business athlete'?"

"I don't think so," said Christopher.

"It's a reference to taking the principles of athletic performance and bringing them into the business world. I correlate practice, like when athletes repeatedly practice being ready for a game, to rhythm. During practice, they're training their muscle memory. In some professions like firefighters, police officers, doctors, and airline pilots, they have training and practice built into their processes."

"I like the idea of becoming the Tiger Woods of the business world. Tell me more," joked Christopher.

"Everything athletes do daily is practice for everything that comes later. Suppose they follow the rules and optimal best practices every time they practice. All future engagements or assignments become that much more routine and muscle memory takes over, which increases effectiveness and efficiency. That's why it's important to follow a good rhythm to sink in the concepts of data, economy, tools, alignment, integration, lead, and leverage, and having that right strategy. None of those are onetime activities. They need to be practiced repeatedly on a daily, monthly, and weekly basis."

"I see what you're getting at," said Christopher. "We try to implement habits to keep up regularly with our processes and programs, but when you put it in terms of rhythm, it makes a little more sense."

"One of the simplest and most effective items that reinforce rhythm is implementing daily huddles. I like 15-minute daily huddles first thing in the morning. This way, your team can discuss top priorities, the KPI status, and any places where someone might be stuck waiting for another team member to deliver something else."

"We have little snags like that all the time," said Christopher.

"Most companies do. When you discuss your top three priorities, the other team members stay up-to-date on your progress. But when you also discuss snags and stuck points, it creates a synergetic form of accountability across the different teams. If the marketing team is waiting on your approval, for example, you might be delaying them for something that should only take you a few minutes to approve. These meetings clarify and fight off friction in the workplace."

"That makes sense, and the top three things for the day reminds me of one of the first recommendations you gave me," said Christopher as the cart came to a stop.

"Exactly," said Ford. "I think you see how a lot of my methods interconnect. In addition to daily meetings, it's also important to have weekly staff meetings, monthly strategic discussions, quarterly business reviews, and annual strategic plans."

Christopher placed his tee in the ground. "Do all these meetings have a different objective?"

"They're all a little different, but one thing remains the same. Whether you're meeting once a day or once a year, you always want to start with a good news portion. This could be the results from the previous meeting or even news like one of your co-workers celebrating a baby. Not only is it positive, but saying something good fights off the negative instincts to start with something that went wrong. A lot of us in business want to get down to solving problems or fixing things, and things that need fixing tend to be negative, but this good news update makes it a habit to start meetings with the positive."

"We've definitely had our share of meetings that started bad and then just lead to feeding frenzies of finger-pointing and everyone getting defensive."

"That's not good for anyone," said Ford.

"So, what's different about weekly compared to daily meetings?" asked Christopher.

Ford began, "Weekly updates start with good news and review KPIs, but then they transition into things like status reports for corporate rocks, basic client needs reviews, team member issues, round table discussions and critiques of best practices, and cascading messages from the team to clarity or define unified commitment across different teams within the company. This meeting should be about an hour or so."

"These sound like our weekly staff meetings and should be slightly bigger picture than the daily huddles?"

"In a sense," said Ford. "Then, there's the Monthly Strategic. Again, start with good news, but transition to the monthly financial review, discuss key company issues, and make decisions on those issues. Break down key strategic items that drive the company forward so you don't stop something that's working for you, and again, drive the total commitment factor across the teams. This meeting might take one or two hours."

"Sounds like it's a little more data-driven to some degree," said Christopher.

"Somewhat, yes. But data is used in all aspects of the meetings as well," replied Ford. "Then there's the Quarterly Business Review. Every three months, you want to discuss good news, review your quarterly rocks, take a deep dive into your financial review, brainstorm key strategic business items, set rocks for the following quarter, and confirm commitment across the board. This meeting should also around two to four hours."

Christopher nodded.

"It is also important to note that all meetings, except the huddles, end with a wrap-up and cascading messages agreement. The wrap-up serves two purposes. One to confirm actionable items—or to-do's—and two, to allow all team members a closing thought. All actionable items should be captured in writing and include who is accountable, who is participating, and any commitment dates. With the cascading messages agreement, it's important to align all participants around how the agreement will be communicated to sub-teams and all colleagues regarding the topics and actions discussed."

"I see," said Christopher.

"Sometimes, the whole meeting might be confidential, and only some of the items will be communicated outside of the meeting room. More important than agreeing to what is communicated is agreeing how it is communicated."

"How does that work exactly?"

"For example," began Ford. "Let's say a customer situation requires multiple teams to work the weekend. The reason for the overtime needs to be constantly communicated across groups. You don't want one team told that the reason was, 'Sue screwed up' and another team being told 'the client is a jerk, so we have work overtime.' Even if this is true, it does not matter and shouldn't be communicated. You would want to make sure all teams understand the importance of the client and that the client has a commitment to one of their suppliers. Thus, they are not able to wait another week for delivery."

"Keep up the morale. Focus on the problem and solution rather than pointing fingers."

"Right," said Ford. "Then, finally, there's the Annual Strategic Meeting. Once a year, it's a good idea to discuss how you performed for the year and make adjustments to both tactics and strategy, as necessary."

"These I know about," said Christopher. "When we first met, we were doing a strategy session. That was not long ago."

"Feels like we have known each other for years, with all the golf we have been playing," said Ford. "Yearly, the long-term strategy may or may not change, but it is important that you confirm things. Annually, it is important to set the big rocks for the year, set new targets and metrics, discuss strategic programs. After we finished the strategy for the year, we then confirmed the budget for the following year[1]."

"So, were you serious when you said you were thinking about coming out of retirement to do some consulting part-time?" asked Christopher.

"I'm kicking around the idea," Ford shrugged. "Spending time with you and talking about what's been happening with work lately has made me think it's a good plan."

---

[1] Visit www.aspensummitgroup.com/details to download a rhythm schedule summary.

"I agree," said Christopher. "Let me know if you decide you're gonna do it. If you need anything from me, you know I'm your guy."

Ford laughed. "Got it."

Before he cranked his vehicle, Christopher pulled out his notebook and recorded his notes on the Rhythm of Business based on his conversation with Ford.

RHYTHM OF BUSINESS NOTES

1. Tie everything together with rhythm.
    - Rhythm creates habits of best practices
    - Rhythm creates muscle memory that enforces efficiency
    - Practice like a business athlete to take advantage of the spacing effect

2. Utilize the following meeting rhythm.
    - Daily Huddles
    - Weekly tactical
    - Monthly strategic thinking
    - Quarterly business reviews
    - Annual strategic planning sessions

3. Use these meeting best practices.
    - Start with good news
    - Confirm actions and accountability before the meeting's end
    - Confirm cascading messages before the meeting's end

CHAPTER 11

THE RESULTS

- There are no secrets to success. It is the result of preparation, hard work, and learning from failure.
  - Colin Powell

- Successful people ask better questions, and as a result, they get better answers.
  - Tony Robbins

- Insanity: doing the same thing over and over again and expecting different results.
  -Albert Einstein

Christopher and his wife Michelle returned home after an afternoon of mountain biking in the hills. After dinner that night, he sat at his desk, sent out a couple of emails, and took out his notebook. He wanted to refresh his memory on the notes he'd taken from his discussions with Ford these past few weeks.

Set a **Strategy**

Focus on what is important

Incorporate **Data** to drive decision and processes

Have a solid **Economic** plan for the company

Invest in **Training** the team and equipping them with the right **tools.**

Align the organization

Integrate the human systems

Lead and **Leverage** the teams (and his) time and skills

Apply a business **Rhythm** to the focus.

He looked twice at the page and chuckled. "I'm going to have to ask him if he did that on purpose," Christopher muttered to himself.

He realized the first letter of each focus area spelled **DETAILS.**

Focusing on the DETAILS with Rhythm = Success

Christopher texted Ford Monday morning with his discovery.

"You caught me," replied Ford in a text message. "My method does spell DETAILS!"

The duo continued to play golf every weekend, but the conversations tended to be more traditional such as golf, family, movies, and restaurant recommendations rather than work topics.

As the months passed and the team implemented Ford's recommendations, Christopher and the board noticed that revenue was up, profits increased, and there was less friction.

Christopher invited Ford to visit the office for a small gathering to meet more of the team.

"Right this way, Mr. Ford," said Kim as she escorted Ford into Christopher's office.

"Glad you could make it," said Christopher. "I know your schedule is likely filling up with new clients now that you're back in the game."

Ford laughed. "There are a few new contacts in my phone, but I like to keep my schedule fairly open for golf games," he joked as he shook Christopher's hand.

Christopher showed Ford around the office, and then the duo stopped by the break room to grab a cold beer from the new four-tap beer dispenser in the office lounge.

"Christopher, I cc'd you on the memo about next week's events, but I think Joselyn has everything covered for the marketing and events," said Kim. "If there's nothing else, I'm going to grab a drink and prep for next week's QBRs," she said.

"Please do. Sounds like a plan," he responded. "Thanks, Kim."

"Next week is our QBR, and I'm looking forward to the energy they bring to the organization," Christopher added.

"So, what do your days look like now?" asked Ford as he tossed his left foot on his right knee.

"My days start with one of the first pieces of advice you ever mentioned to me: to have my top three priorities for each day. I love that practice and thought process. Most days, I'm working on my perform activities from the D.E.P. chart."

"Delegation?" asked Ford.

"I have delegated and let go of the items that don't best leverage me for the organization. We have had one or two colleagues exit the company, but it was for the best for both parties. These days, I can finally focus on the tech and key customers and not what kind of beer we have for office events," said Christopher.

"Don't underestimate the power of free beer," joked Ford. "It was free beer that convinced me to help you hang that oversized flat-screen on your patio."

"Sure," said Christopher with a smile, "but that's just one of the many details that run this office."

"Tell me some of the others," responded Ford. "You're my latest testimonial after all."

"Sure. Happy to do so. When we focused on DATA, we created accountability, and with increased transparency, everyone can see what works and what doesn't work. We have three times more dashboards with KPIs down to the individual. Our meetings are more productive, with increased responsiveness and insight.

"Most importantly, is this: no one feels like they're just spinning their wheels. Every action is either process or an experiment for a better future action."

Ford nodded.

"With ECONOMICS, we were able to invest more in our business. We're working on building up cash flow, but just the mindset of cash flow and return on capital helps many of our smaller decisions and provides somewhat of a singular focus to know where to invest and where to wait or ignore."

Ford approved once more.

"With TOOLS and TRAINING, we worked on processes rather than trying every new tool in the market. Everyone on the team understands their part within the customer journey, the colleague affiliations, and the overall company. More importantly, this helps the overall team work together in synergy."

A few team members joined the table and sat around Christopher and Ford with fresh cold ones.

"With ALIGNMENT, we were able to focus on the overall navigation of the company, which meant finding the balance between firm goals and flexible paths. This means being transparent but also communicating daily with leaders and team members."

11 | The Results

"Slack and in-person," chimed in a new hire to Christopher's right.

"With INTEGRATION, we hired Joselyn. She works on our incentive programs, which means small events like this one, but she also worked on finding a better insurance plan for the team. We also noticed an increase in our sprint success, and team trust is way up."

"With direct, real-time, meaningful feedback," said Joselyn as she entered the circle.

Christopher continued, "With LEAD and LEVERAGE, the biggest advantage has perhaps been removing roadblocks. We stopped some micromanagement to let the team make their own decisions," he said.

Ford and the team laughed.

"As for our STRATEGY, that's somewhat changed given the data. But we continue to focus on the purpose of the company, our big rocks, and our WAG, which remains in our sights," said Christopher.

"There's a reason why strategy comes first, even though it tails the acronym," joked Ford. "Your strategy is the vision, and everything else is the blueprint on how to build the house itself. Any other thoughts before I kick your butt on that Ping-Pong table?" asked Ford.

"Every day we focus on the details with rhythm," replied the protégé. "I have never forgotten the analogy you shared of harnessing the power of the sun. My father, who was in the military, would call the APEX system a 'force multiplier' for a company's success."

"I like that, but I'm not familiar with that expression," said Ford. "What exactly is a force multiplier?"

"A force multiplier is anything that amplifies the input to increase the output," responded Christopher. "We had a lot of success at HealthCloud with our share of growth challenges, but as they apply the APEX system, we are seeing additional exponential benefits in other areas of our performance. Right now, the whole organization is aligned, focused, and on track to hit our major goals.

"Glad to hear it," Ford responded. "Now, I've got twenty bucks that says I can kick your butt at Ping-Pong."

"You're on!" responded Christopher.

THANK YOU FOR READING THIS BOOK. I HOPE YOU FOUND IT HELPFUL.

Writing this book was more difficult than I thought it would be. In the beginning, I spent a great deal of time overthinking the process, and then I remembered three pieces of advice I give my clients:

- The only person standing between you and success is you.
- Perfect is the enemy of done.
- And as General George Patton said, "A good plan, violently executed now, is better than a perfect plan next week."

So, I took my own advice and finished the damn thing (my second book can be perfect, but for now, on with the show).

IMPLEMENTING THE SYSTEM

If you've already begun to apply some of these principles to your business, congratulations! You have taken the most important step—starting.

If you have not yet begun to implement the APEX methodology, below are a few suggestions for moving forward.

Whether you read this book cover to cover (or jumped ahead to the end), I want to reiterate how important each step in the process is for your business.

- Data is important
- Economics is important
- Training is important
- Alignment is important
- Integration is important
- Leadership is important
- Strategy is important
- Focusing is important
- Rhythm is important

Some of the chapter principles will have a greater impact than others for your particular business, sure, but the DETAILS System is more like chess than checkers. Every piece has its own value toward winning the game. There are many ways to move the pieces and move combinations to win the game.

In addition, there's no shortcut beyond the system itself. Meaning, to get the full force multiplier effect, you need to implement each piece.

How do I select the top 3 areas to begin with? Try one of the following options:

Option A: Select the 3 with the most room for improvement based on the assessment.

Option B: Select the 3 the team believes will deliver the most valuable impact on the organization.

Option C: Do what feels right for your organization. It is more important to begin than to pick the right starting point. You are going to want to optimize them all.

Whichever piece you move first is up to you, but I highly recommend three things:

1. Pick a principle(s) to implement/improve
2. **Focus** on it (commit)
3. Create a **Rhythm** to make it a habit

Tying it in to my golf theme once more, if your ability to putt is excellent but your short game is weak, you must maintain excellent putting, but spend more time on your short game as both are valuable to your overall strategy.

Remember, it is a trek up the mountain—not a sprint—to operational excellence. Focus on what is most important first.

If you want more direct guidance and are truly serious about implementing the full system, maximizing your results in all areas, and building something to last, I encourage you to contact me directly at the link below.

www.aspensummitgroup.com/details

ACTIVE PERFORMANCE EXECUTION

Are you interested in learning more about the APEX methodology?

Would you like assistance implementing the methods and tactics associated with Focusing on the DETAILS with Rhythm?

Do you realize the benefits of getting unstuck and focusing on the DETAILS with Rhythm?

Contact Andy Vassallo, join the mailing list, and download a sample workbook to go along with this book at the link below.

www.aspensummitgroup.com/details

Focus on the DETAILS with Rhythm:

- Focus (Strategy, Alignment, Prioritization, and Clarity)
- Details (Blocking and Tackling)
- Rhythm (Consistency and Focus)

Andy believes exceptional breakthrough results come from working with teams. Transformation happens with the whole team, not individual change.

What To Expect Working With Andy

- Teams will be held accountable
- Expect a participatory method
- Be asked a lot of questions
- Hear the hard truths
- Get sh*t done
- Learn the secret of ***Focusing on the DETAILS with Rhythm***

ANDY VASSALLO BIOGRAPHY

Andy Vassallo is an executive advisor, consultant, author, and the creator of the APEX Methodology (Active Performance Execution) and the DETAILS System, **The Focused CEO: Why some organizations thrive and some spin their wheels**

Andy is known for his big picture point-of-view. He's able to see opportunities for improvement and risk points in a variety of industries to pinpoint problems and diagnose solutions. Along with the enterprise-wide view, his technology background makes him adept with details. Couple these traits with his direct, transparent, and imaginative style, and you'll understand why he is a proven Get-Sh*t-Done advisor and consultant.

As a consultant, he brings over 30 years of executive leadership, management consulting, professional services, outsourcing, and information technology (IT) experience in assisting his clients. His experience includes executive leadership at companies ranging from entrepreneur start-ups, Venture back groups, and large multibillion-dollar Fortune 100 companies.

As an entrepreneur, his journey began in the Detroit suburbs when he purchased a Commodore 64 computer and tried to convince a family friend who was an accountant to join forces and write a computer program to do their taxes. Unfortunately, that venture never took off, but lessons were learned.

After college and a few years of writing code and working as a software engineer in Boston and San Diego, Andy joined with three friends to start a company in the California Bay Area, just north of the Silicon Valley in the 1990s. Jumping ahead a few years, we find Andy in a leadership position at a pre-IPO healthcare consulting firm, just as that company was poised for great things.

Over the next 12+ years, that company, Superior Consultant, grew exponentially with high client satisfaction and recognition as an outstanding place to work. Andy was a key leader in the company's success as its IPO led it to a NASDAQ top 5% performance. As the leader of the provider healthcare consulting group, he oversaw 400+ consultants and a P&L of over $100 million.

After working with Superior, Andy's career included executive and C-level positions at a Fortune 250, a Fortune 100 company, two private equity-backed firms, and two additional start-ups.

During his career working in Boston, San Diego, San Francisco, Denver, and Michigan, Andy worked with genuinely genius-level technology experts and innovational leaders. While working with them, he was able to absorb a portion of their vast knowledge.

Over the course of those thirty growth years, through three economic dips (the Y2K dip, the 2008 recession, and the COVID pandemic), Andy developed the APEX methodology for active performance excellence.

Focus on the DETAILS with Rhythm:

Andy currently resides in Northville, Michigan, with his wife and two adult children. On most weekends, weather permitting, you can find him on the golf course. If you want to increase your company's performance through strategic execution by focusing on the DETAILS with Rhythm, connect with Andy on LinkedIn or at www.aspensummitgroup.com. .

ACKNOWLEDGMENTS

I would like to start by thanking my awesome and loving wife, Åsa. Thank you for providing the support and time to finish this project.

I also want to acknowledge my children, Ashley and Andrew, who remind me every day what it is like to be young. May they someday realize I have advice worth listening to.

And my mother, Connie. Thank you for a lifetime of support and for teaching me the value of generosity.

In memory of my father, Joseph, a man who truly knew someone every place he went. Thank you for teaching me the value of hard work.

I want to give special thanks to Richard Helppie for providing insight and notes into this process. During my 12+ years at Superior Consultant, I learned and practiced some of the foundations of APEX methodology. Richard has provided years of mentorship on principle-driven management and continues to be a friend to this day.

Acknowledgments

Thank you to Dann L., Don R., Mike M., Rich H., Mitch P., Steve Gand, Gene G., who took the time to read drafts and provide notes and suggestions.

Thank you to my colleagues throughout the years who have provided knowledge and inspiration during my whole career.

An extra thank you to those I worked with at IDX, Global Works, and Superior Consultant. Those were the days!

Thank you to the team at Happy Self-Publishing for the details that helped me complete this project.

APEX QUESTIONNAIRE

The following assessment will analyze your company's progress in each category listed in the book: Strategy, Focus, Data, Economics, Tools, Alignment, Integration, Lead, and Rhythm.

You may find that your organization is stronger in some categories than others, but these questionnaires should provide a guide as to where you should start.

To get the most accurate results, it is critical to provide honest, realistic answers to see where you can grow as an organization.

As you answer these questions, please use the following numerical system to best understand your company's current position and availability for growth and maximum impact. The answers are listed in terms of 5 being highly positive and 1 being very negative.

Big Yes, always and/or everyone	5 points
Yes, mostly and/or most people	4 points
Don't know or unsure	2 points
No, some and/or most people no	1 point
Big No, always and/or everyone no	0 points

What is the difference between *Yes* and B*ig Yes*? I like to differentiate between *Yes* and B*ig Yes* as thinking of *Big Yes* as the same as *Hell Yes*. If you can answer *Hell Yes* to a question, you get a *Big Yes*.

As an example, and for clarity, notice the difference between the following:

Question:
Would everyone like a free million dollars?

The answer would be *Hell Yes* or *Big Yes* for 5 points.

Question:
Is a football field 100 yards?

The answer to this question would be *Yes*. We can safely assume **most, but not all,** people would answer *Yes*.

One additional way to differentiate between *Yes* and *Big Yes* is that to have a *Big Yes*, 99% of the people in the organization would answer *Yes* to the questions, and a normal *Yes* is if 60 %-98% of the people would answer *Yes*.

Remember, it takes a team to change, not just one person. The dialogue around these topics and the transparency of the open exchange of ideas is an important first step of the change process. Let's begin…

Strategy Assessment

1. Can your company's annual strategic plan fit onto one page (front and back)?
2. Does your company's strategic plan include a clear statement of what your company does and what gives it a strategic advantage over your competition (i.e., a strong value proposition)?
3. Has the strategic plan been clearly communicated to ALL colleagues, multiple times, and through multiple methods?
4. All colleagues can accurately state the vision, strategy, and goals in the strategic plan?
5. Does your company's strategic plan include the top three prioritized "rocks," or initiatives and goals for the company broken up by quarter?

Focus Assessment

1. Do you write down the three most important tasks for the day, and are you focusing on them until they're finished?
2. Do you have a clear #1 priority daily?
3. Are colleagues providing clear, actionable, and measurable accountability updates?
4. Are you leveraging the power of the sun in that all colleagues have a sense of urgency and involvement as to what is important every day?
5. Are you tracking and publicly reporting daily focused scorecards?

Data Assessment

1. Does every person in the company have a KPI?
2. Are scorecards visible and used daily?
3. Is data being used in everyday decisions and for process improvement?
4. Are you tracking predictive metrics?
5. Are you drilling into the data and asking "Why" three (3) times on a routine basis?

Economics Assessment

1. Do you have 6-12 months of cash on hand?
2. Do you know your company's cash flow levers?
3. Do you know your return on capital spent?
4. Is your team aligned around steady improvement, or are they focusing on hockey stick forecasts?
5. Do you have P&L accountability with all line items in the P&L assigned to an accountable business owner?

Tools & Training Assessment

1. Are your colleagues knowledgeable on how/why the business operates?
2. Do you optimize your best-practice methods before purchasing new tools?
3. Are colleagues educated on behavioral and technical skills?
4. Is there a culture of ongoing learning that exists within the company?

5. Have you created a single source of truth for key metrics?

Alignment Assessment

1. Does your executive team have trust and transparency?
2. Is everyone comfortable engaging in productive conflict on critical issues?
3. Do all colleagues know the aligning message for the quarter/year?
4. Are all colleagues aligned and driving to the #1 priority for the quarter?
5. Are the 3 Cs balanced when making decisions?

Integration Assessment

1. Does every colleague have a PEP (personal energy) plan?
2. Is healthy behavior integrated into the review process?
3. Is colleagues' feedback (reviews) provided throughout the year in real-time and NOT provided once a year?
4. Are the incentive programs aligned across teams and at all levels?
5. Is healthy behavior part of the hiring, promotion, and termination process?

Lead & Leverage Assessment

1. Is leadership's time appropriate for the D.E.P. (Delegate, Educate, Perform) chart?
2. Are leaders eliminating roadblocks, not creating hurdles?
3. Are you using the start/stop exercises to gather feedback from your team members?
4. Are you spending a good portion of your leadership time outside of your office and invested in meaningful dialogue with colleagues?
5. Is leadership leading by example in all areas of culture and performance?

Rhythm Assessment

1. Are daily huddle meetings used by all teams within the company?
2. Are meetings concluded with a confirmed agreement on actions, assignments, and cascading messages?
3. Are you allocating time for the leadership team to have strategic discussions and planning?
4. Are you conducting a leadership QBR to reinforce accountability and focus?
5. Are you conducting an annual two-day off-site strategic planning session?

Get Your Results:

Add your points per section.

Over 20 points in a section: Congratulations! You are ready to move on to the advanced concepts and application of that section of the APEX method.

Under 20 points in a section: You will see a significant improvement in productivity and achievement when you implement APEX methods for that area.

For a custom team assessment and facilitated discussion, contact Andy at the following link:

www.aspensummitgroup.com/details

If you decided to move forward with implementing all or some of the APEX method, the following are some suggested group discussion starters. These suggestions assume the assessment was given to a leadership team.

The topics can be discussed in any order.

- Do you have a solid starting strategy? If not, why? Strategy is always the starting point.
- What three (3) sections scored the highest? Why for each?
- What three (3) sections scored the lowest? Why for each?
- What three (3) sections have the largest spread between the answers of the team? Why?
- Was there a difference between how the CEO views things and how the team views things? If

yes, how large? Why? If no, does the team think bias crept into the assessment?

- What three (3) sections do the team feel would have the largest impact on performance? Why?
- Does the team think the APEX and DETAILS method would be positively accepted by the organization? Why or why not?

THANK YOU

Thank You For Reading My Book!

I really appreciate all of your feedback, and I love hearing what you have to say.

I need your input to make the next version of this book and my future books even better.

Please leave me a helpful review on Amazon letting me know what you thought of the book.

Thank you so much!
Andy Vassallo

www.ingramcontent.com/pod-product-compliance
Lightning Source LLC
Chambersburg PA
CBHW020658220526
45464CB00001B/481